THE DIVINE CURE FOR A BROKEN HEART

With love from
Abiodun Onnelukami
(Mrs. O)

THE DIVINE CURE FOR A BROKEN HEART

✦

KEYS TO TREASURE

Dr. Elu Akpala Onnekikami

iUniverse, Inc.
New York Lincoln Shanghai

THE DIVINE CURE FOR A BROKEN HEART
KEYS TO TREASURE

iUniverse books may be ordered through booksellers or by contacting:

iUniverse
2021 Pine Lake Road, Suite 100
Lincoln, NE 68512
www.iuniverse.com
1-800-Authors (1-800-288-4677)

All scripture quotations are taken from the authorized King James and the Amplified version of the Bible. All stories in this book are true, for privacy reasons, some names and places were changed.

ISBN-13: 978-0-595-37878-4 (pbk)
ISBN-13: 978-0-595-82249-2 (ebk)
ISBN-10: 0-595-37878-1 (pbk)
ISBN-10: 0-595-82249-5 (ebk)

Printed in the United States of America

This book is dedicated to my Lord and savior, Jesus Christ. Also, to all who have experienced hurt in any form and would like to feel completely healed and resurrected.

Contents

Acknowledgments

Words are inadequate to express my profound gratitude to the leader of our ministry, my spiritual mentor and brother, Alex O. Akpala, for his God led wisdom and spiritual insights that enabled me to tackle this issue.

If I have to write down the names of every one who have ever forgiven me it would be a very long list. I thank them all for helping me learn about forgiveness. For those who might still hold resentments for what I have done or for what I have failed to do and I am not aware of it, please forgive me.

I am grateful to Arinze Alinnor for his great contribution to this project. Thank you, my friend and fellow vine-yard laborer for your commitment of carefully stewarding this life changing message.

I would also like to extend my sincere gratitude to Romiwa Akpala Onnekikami for taking the time from his hectic then final year law school program to edit and give invaluable suggestions to this project. Thank you son, the Lord loves you and your immeasurable efforts are appreciated.

Preface

"A Broken Heart" it is one of the most painful emotional experiences one can ever have, whether it is from a severed relationship or the death of a loved one. Everyone has to deal with a broken heart at some point in life because we live in a fallen world and as a result we are constantly faced with shattered dreams, unexpected losses and hurting relationships.

Song writers over the years have tried to capture this heart wrenching feelings that arises from these circumstances with lyrics like; "How I am supposed to live without you when all I have been living for is gone," How do I know if you really love me", "You have lost that loving feeling", to mention but a few. Most often these emotions are not articulated as precisely as we often wish they were. Most of the time the pain is so deep and so excruciating that we tend to repress and deny the anguish rather than handle it properly.

> We live in a fallen world and as a result we are constantly faced with shattered dreams, unexpected losses and hurting relationships.

To aid our healing process, we often look to prayers. Most of us have prayed all sorts of prayers. We expect immediate answers to these prayers but are often left lying in wait. We become perplexed as to why our prayers and dreams remain unrealized. Many have blamed their continued frustrations on God's Word, which they received, nevertheless did not come to pass as they anticipated. While evaluating this conundrum I have discovered that the seed itself (God's Word) was not the problem but rather where the seed was sown.

Would you like to get closer to God? Would you like to know how to heal that broken heart? Would you like to have spiritual prosperity? Would you like to have financial prosperity in your life? Are you in need of God's healing for other illnesses? Have you sometimes wondered why you have been tithing to your churches and different ministries and are not receiving your harvest? Would you like to know how to eliminate the enemy designed obstacles that might be preventing you from getting these God promised blessings? If your answer to any of these questions is YES, then get ready to receive this awesome message. It will not only enlighten and renew your world; it will empower you and show you how to reach your divine-promised destiny.

A few years ago, we moved into a house, which was a fixer upper. The house had not been occupied for about six months. As one would expect, it lacked TLC—TENDER-LOVING-CARE.

The front lawn was extremely bad. The grass was withered and discolored. Curled leaves and broken tree branches added to the unpleasant scenery. It was highly embarrassing. The lawn was by far the worst on the block. It was during this period that God started implanting this message of forgiveness and prosperity in my heart. I knew that I needed to do

> It will empower you and show you how to reach your divine-promised destiny.

something; at the very least, to have a decent lawn like everyone else on the street.

I wanted my own lawn to have the sort of beautiful green grass you see on a football or soccer field. That was the desired objective. After consultation with some lawn experts, we decided that we needed to uproot all the old grass and plant new seeds. So we cleaned up the lawn, dumped all the dead grass and other garbage in the dumpster. Then we tilled the soil and added manure. The manure's odor was almost unbearable, but it did not matter since it was what was needed to accomplish my objective. We added fertilizer and then planted the new seeds.

After a few months of watering twice a day and sunlight from above, I now have one of the best lawns on the street. This is exactly what you need to do to get God-promised healing and prosperity in your life. In this short story, there are three requirements for seeds to grow when they are planted. It needs good soil, water and sunlight. You need to dig deep down into yourself in order to check out any trace of unforgiveness that might be in you. Be ready to confess it and then LET IT GO. For you to get your broken heart healed and anticipate your God promised harvest, you need to have forgiveness, love and patience. These are the ideal steps toward your healing and prosperity. Go through this book and decide to let it go.

"The Lord is close to the brokenhearted and saves those who are crushed in spirit."...King David (Psalm 34 v 12)

"If we practice an eye for an eye and a tooth for a tooth, soon the whole world will be blind and toothless."—Mahatma Gandhi

1

What Is Forgiveness?

Forgiveness is an act of God's grace; to forget permanently and not hold people of faith accountable for sins they confess. To a lesser degree, it is the gracious human act of not holding a wrong act against a person. Forgiveness is also the gracious act of God by which believers are made right with God. Forgiveness is not based on merit, but on grace and love.

Unforgiveness is a spiritual death. When we forgive completely we move from spiritual death to spiritual life through Jesus Christ our Lord. Spiritual death is worst than physical death. When you are spiritually dead, you are a dead man or woman walking. But the good news for us is that we can rise from our spiritual death at any moment to a choice of a spiritual life.

Complete forgiveness is the key. You must forgive all manners of past hurt and grudges. This will allow you to walk into the spiritual life of healing and prosperity obtainable through Jesus Christ by forgiveness.

Some people have problems with the idea of forgiveness. These people believe forgiveness does not take the harm of sin seriously. But I will attest that forgiveness takes sin very seriously. Forgiveness does not simply excuse sin by saying, "O that's alright, your sin really wasn't bothersome, or my stay in the hospital wasn't that long, besides, I was able to catch up on my reading!" No, forgiveness calls sin exactly what it is, sin. In many ways it holds the sinner accountable for their actions. Forgiveness says, "You hurt me, and what you did was wrong, but I will not hold it against you. I will not try to get back at you and I will not hate you for it.

Forgiveness initiates the healing process. You have probably heard someone say, or even said to yourself, "I'll forgive them when they come and say they are sorry." This is not God's way. God said, "I forgive you". Now will you accept it by confessing and repenting?" If we wait for a confession before we forgive, most often, the wait will be for a long time.

In the book, "What's so amazing about Grace," Philip Yancey describes a story about a husband and wife who had an argument about dinner preparation. The argument was so heated that the couple slept in separate rooms. Neither one approached the other to apologize or to offer forgiveness. As a result of this rather petty issue they remained in separate rooms' years after the argument. Each night they would go to bed hoping the other would approach them with an apology or forgiveness but to no avail. Their lack of forgiveness and stubbornness ultimately sabotaged their marriage.

> Some behaviors need to be excused rather than forgiven.

God's forgiveness does not wait for repentance; it initiates and calls out repentance by offering forgiveness. This is why some people have great difficulty forgiving others. Fearing confrontation, these people remain remorseless and fail to do the hard work required for forgiveness.

Some wrongs against us are not serious enough to warrant forgiveness. Some behavior needs to be excused rather than forgiven. Accidents, mistakes, minor lapses in judgment, and misunderstandings seldom need forgiveness; usually they just need to be excused. I know about two elderly brothers who were in a car accident some years ago. Each blamed the other for the accident. The one driving said his brother was distracting him, and the other brother said it was due to bad driving. Both should have said, "These things happen" and then proceeded with their lives, but instead of excusing each other, they have not spoken in years.

It is not easy to give up our right to be hurt, to be angry, to get back, and to hate the other for what they have done. You may have had terrible things done to you by someone you loved and trusted which hurt you and broke your trust. You may have also lost a great deal because of someone's actions and your heart is full of pain. I believe that unforgiveness can act as a cancer, eating up our entire being, and serving as an obstacle to our prosperity. The ability which allows us to tap into the divine grace of God and expunge from our heart every root of hurt and bitterness is FORGIVENESS.

"And when you stand to pray, forgive whatever you may hold against any one, so that your heavenly father may also forgive your sins."...Lord Jesus Christ (Mark 25 v12)

"When you hold resentment towards another, you are bound to that person or condition by an emotional link that is stronger than steel. Forgiveness is the only way to dissolve that link and get free"...Catherine Ponder

2

The Cost of Forgiveness

The rather painful cost of forgiveness is best illustrated with the parable Jesus Christ told his disciples concerning the wealthy King and his debtor, as found in the book of Matthew chapter 18 verses 23-35

In the King's line up was an absolutely terrified debtor who would rather face an angry wife than the King. His debt had become so large that repayment was impossible. The King took one look at the huge sum the man owed and demanded complete payment. The infuriated King refused to listen to any excuses, and told his guards "Sell him, his wife, and his children on the slave market. We will get what we can." The man probably thought about his lovely wife, beautiful children and threw himself to the King, "I realize that I have not done the right thing by not paying my debt to you. Give me time and I will repay everything I owe you."

The King stared at the humbled man for few moments and probably due to the wife and children forgave him for all his debts. I suspect that the man did not even stop for a cup of coffee. He must have busted into his house and proclaimed "We are free".

Make no mistake that the wealthy King Jesus eluded to is God. We have in effect; all stood before God's court of judgment and heard him say, "You owe me infinite amounts of righteousness, for that is what is required of you." No single person could repay a debt of this magnitude. No matter how hard we try, none of us can impress God with our goodness. So God, through the death of Jesus Christ, freely forgave our sins.

The King in the parable freely forgave his debtor, just as God has freely forgiven us. Therefore, forgiveness is essentially as free as the air we breathe. God gives forgiveness freely to repentant sinners, because the debts of our sins were fully paid when Jesus Christ died on the cross in our place.

The question then becomes how does this apply when we forgive one another? For example, a man commits adultery and his wife forgives him. She absorbs the loss when she forgives. The one who is sinned against bears it in their body, their emotions, their spirit, the brunt of sin committed against them. Because she cares, she has the right and ability to do as the King did, forgive. Always bear in mind that the standard of forgiveness was set when Jesus died for us at the cross.

Let us take another look at the cost of forgiveness in this parable. After the debtor had been completely forgiven, he went out after someone who owed him a small amount. It was small debt, the type you might owe a friend because you ran out cash on a trip, let's assume fifty dollars as an example. Instead of having mercy on his debtor, the man who was forgiven by the king threw his friend in prison for the little amount of money owed.

> Always bear in mind that the standard of forgiveness was set when Jesus died for us at the cross.

When the King found out, he summoned the man whom he had previously forgiven and said: "You wicked slave; I forgave you all your debts because you pleaded with me. Should you not also have mercy on your fellow slave, even as I had mercy on you?" And the King handed the man over to be tortured until he would repay that which he had once been forgiven. Yes, the cost of forgiveness is great, but was paid dearly with the Lord's life. Never forget this fact and learn to move on no matter how painful the cost. Limit the damage; otherwise the cost of holding on to that unforgiveness might cost you more in a many other ways. The next story here might inspire you to let it go.

Ebuwa's eldest son, Joseph, who was twenty-one years old, and his fiancée, Beth, had just moved from New York City to Long beach, California. Late one evening, both young people were instantly killed when their car was struck by a drunk driver. Joseph's mother, Susan Ebuwa, experienced such unbearable grief that she often found herself walking the streets late at night sobbing and screaming.

The drunk driver, David was charged with first degree murder. In a normal situation, the typical charge is a lesser offense such as manslaughter. However, Susan sought for a murder conviction due to the mental pain and suffering she was experiencing. The twenty-two year old drunk driver pleaded guilty and waived his right to trial. He was guilt ridden and wanted to die.

Given this scenario, the cost of forgiveness seemed too much to ask of Susan Ebuwa. Touched by the Holy Spirit, a miraculous event unfolded in the court room as the accused was sentenced to fifteen years to life.

In that instant, Susan realized that David was not the monster every one made her believe. She realized that he also had parents who loved him. She proclaimed to the court that "David did not commit murder; it was just a tragic accident." She then rose from her seat, walked past the guards and gave David a hug.

Susan began to work tirelessly to have David's sentence and charges reduced to manslaughter. After serving seven years in prison and due to Susan's continuous efforts, David was released on parole.

The cost of forgiveness for Susan was the immense mental anguish she endured. Forgiving David required Susan to look past her own struggles and frustrations. She had to reach deep within and consider another's suffering that would occur from a life conviction. Susan and David both realized the power of forgiveness that day in the court room, and now they can both share this experience with others around the world.

"Do away with all quarrelling, rage, anger, insults and every kind of malice: be good and understanding, mutually forgiving one another as God forgave you in Christ…Apostle Paul (Ephesians 4 v 31-32)

"When we are a forgiving people, our past loose their strangle hold on the present and we are free to follow God without the chains of bitterness and malice choking our every thought and actions."

3

The Power of Forgiveness

Forgiveness is a foundational principle of Christianity, yet one of the very things that holds many in bondage today.

I want to let you know that no matter what sins you have committed, our God is a great and merciful God. He allows u-turns in our spiritual journey here on earth, and is ready to forgive you as long as you forgive others. Have you ever been driving or been a passenger in a car? And while driving on the freeway or highway, missed your intended exit or just missed your direction because you were in deep thoughts. Maybe you were listening to some great music by your favorite artist. Or you were having a great conversation with your friend or spouse, or maybe you were having an argument and as a result you missed your direction or intended exit.

What do you do when you realize you have just missed your exit or your direction? You have to immediately get off on the next off ramp so that you can make adjustments and proceed to your desired destination.

This is the same thing we must do in our own spiritual journey when we find ourselves on the wrong spiritual freeway exit, or when we miss our spiritual direction. Our distractions in failing to reach our desired spiritual exit or direction might be the result of devil-designed obstacles, which we are bound to see frequently in our lifetime.

The good news today is that in our Lord's spiritual freeway, and through the power contained in forgiveness, He allows us to make that u-turn.

When we pray and ask God for forgiveness, he immediately put us on the right spiritual direction and our right to prosperity is released.

While gathering resources for this book, the Lord led me to an article in the Newsweek issue of November 10, 2004, titled, "God and Health". In a recent survey of 1500 people, a researcher at the University of Michigan's School of Public Health found that people who forgive easily tend to enjoy greater psychological well-being and have less depression than those who hold grudges. When you do not forgive you suffer internally. Research upon research has shown that unforgiveness affects your health. Don't let the enemy rob you, through unforgiveness, of your total physical healing and spiritual prosperity.

> In our Lord's spiritual freeway, and through the power contained in forgiveness, He allows us to make that u-turn.

Other news that might interest you, they found that life expectancy in the US is:

If you do not attend church at all you get—75 years

If you attend church less than weekly you get—80 years

If you attend church once per week, you get—82 years.

If you attend church more than weekly, you get—83 years

So go to church every week so that your life expectancy would be at least 82 years.

A true-life story on the power of forgiveness will help drive this awesome message home. In 1902, a family's 19-year-old farm assistance, Alessandro Serenelli attacked Maria Goretti at age 12. He tried to rape Maria, who fought, yelled that it was a sin, and that he would go to hell. He tried to choke her into submission, and then stabbed her fourteen times. She survived in the hospital for two days, forgave her attacker, asked God's forgiveness for him, and died holding a cross. Alessandro was given 30 years in prison for his crime. Initially, he was unrepentant, but claimed that Maria came to him in a vision, offering flowers in forgiveness, and then he became a changed man. Can you imagine how Maria's parents must have felt? Before she died, she told her parents that Alessandro was forgiven. Upon his release from prison, Alessandro immediately went to Maria's mother to beg for forgiveness. The mother forgave him.

Maria Goretti was made a saint, with her mother, brothers, sisters and Alessandro all present. This is an example of the power in forgiveness.

Forgiveness brings healing. It sets one free from the chains, burdens and years of bondage. Have you hated, despised, and begrudged someone for weeks, months and years? Set them free, find relief for yourself, and make brothers of your enemies. Anger and bitterness come as a result of unconfessed and unforgiving transgressions, which in turn may lead to serious health problems. Ulcers, high blood pleasure, migraine headaches and lower back pain can come from concealing our sins and hurts. Karl Menninger, a renowned psychiatrist, once said that if he could convince the patients in psychiatric hospitals that their sins were forgiven, 75% of them could walk out the next day. The power of forgiveness is amazing.

> Forgiveness brings healing. It sets one free from the chains, burdens and years of bondage.

Forgiveness is vital. There is power in forgiveness. It is a revolutionary power; the power of altering, healing and making whole a bruised relationship. If you are a follower of Jesus Christ, you possess, within him, this awesome, profound and revolutionary power.

When the first missionaries came to Alberta, Canada, a young chief of the Cree Indians, named Maskepetoon, savagely opposed them. But he later responded to the gospel and accepted Christ. Shortly afterward, a member of the Blackfoot tribe killed his father. Maskepetoon rode into the village where the murderer lived and demanded that he be brought before him. Confronting the guilty man, he said, "You have killed my father, so now you must be my father. You shall ride my best horse and wear my father's best clothes. Tell your people that this is the way Maskepetoon takes revenge."

In utter amazement and remorse his enemy exclaimed, "My son, now you have killed me!" He meant, of course, that the hate in his own heart had been completely erased by the forgiveness and kindness of the Indian Chief. His father's murderer continued, "Never in the history of my people has such a thing as this been known. My people and all men will say, "The young chief is brave, strong and good. He stands alone."

The book of Romans chapter 12 verses 17-21 voiced:

> "Do not return evil for evil, but let everyone
> see your good will. Do your best to live in peace
> with everybody. Beloved, do not avenge yourselves,
> but let God be the one who punishes, as the Scripture
> says: Vengeance is mine, I will repay says the Lord. And
> It adds: if your enemy is hungry, feed him, if he is thirsty, give
> him something to drink; by doing this you will heap burning coals
> upon his head. Do not let evil defeat you, but conquer evil with
> goodness".

Forgiveness is extremely difficult for humans to do willingly. There are a myriad of reasons not to forgive. To forgive is to absorb the pain of an offense. It means consuming the pain insulated by the associated anger and bitterness, acquitting the offense that caused the pain, and therefore exposing the pain to the light of grace. Forgiveness is an essential to one's well-being.

Not long before she died 1988, in a moment of surprising honesty and before a television audience, Marghanita Laski, a regarded atheist and novelist, said, "What I envy most about you Christians is your forgiveness; I have nobody to forgive me."

According to the latest medical and psychological research, forgiving is beneficial for our soul and our bodies. The research showed that people who forgive experience the following:-

They benefit from a better immune function and lower blood pressure.

They have better mental health than people who do not forgive.

They feel better physically.

They have lower amounts of anger and fewer symptoms of anxiety and depression.

They maintain more satisfying and long-lasting relationships.

Michael McCullough, director of research for the National Institute for Healthcare Research, said, "When we allow ourselves to feel like victims or sit around dreaming up how to retaliate against people who hurt us, these thought patterns take a toll on our mind and bodies.

In the book of Luke chapter 23, our Lord Jesus Christ forgave the people who hammered nailed into his hands, spit at him and eventually killed Him. Forgiving each other is imperative. If we don't, Satan can gain a foothold. Though forgiveness may be difficult, refusing to forgive ultimately leads to hurt, bitterness, anger, resentment, and self-destruction. It tears up families, ruins friendships and worst of all; it can divide a church. I think Satan's most cunning and strongest tactic is to get Christians not to forgive. It simply does not pay to keep record of wrongs or to hold grudges.

There is a Spanish story of a father and son who had become estranged. The son ran away, and the father set off to find him. He searched for months, but to no avail. Finally, in a last effort of desperation, the father put an advert in a Madrid Newspaper. The advert read: "Dear Paco, meet me in front of this Newspaper office at noon on Saturday. All is forgiven. I love you. Your Dad." On that Saturday, 800 Pacos showed up, looking for forgiveness and love from their fathers.

Forgiveness heals relationships. The truth is that any relationship of any depth—from a friend you may not see often but always seem to connect well with, to your best friend, to the marriage relationship itself—all relationships thrive when there is an understanding that forgiveness is an important value to both parties. Why do they thrive? Because, it gives us the freedom not to be perfect. We can make a mistake a misjudgment; we can have a misunderstanding without it being the end of the world or at least the end of the relationship.

Without that freedom, freedom found on forgiveness, we cannot have relationships of any depth or length. Being a forgiving person and a forgiving community, means we give each other the freedom to be ourselves—warts, imperfections, bad moments and all; strengths, beauty and kindness as well.

Another part of the power of forgiveness is its power to release us from bondage. In his book, Lee: The last Years, Charles Flood writes about an incident that happened after the American Civil War. Brigadier General, Robert E. Lee, the son of a Revolutionary War hero, visited a woman from Kentucky after the war. She took him to the remains of a grand, aged tree in front of her house.

> Abundant life happens in part when we let go of the past.

She stood there and wept—bitterly crying that the Federal Artillery fire from the north had destroyed its limbs and trunk. She looked to Lee, expecting him to say something condemning about the north or at least sympathizing with her loss. After just a short silence, Lee said; "Cut it down, my dear Madam, and forget it. It is better to forgive the injustice of the past than to allow them to remain, let not bitterness take root and poison the rest of your life."

We like to nurse grudges sometimes, don't we? So-and-so did this to me and so-and-so did that. Sometimes they are small offenses and sometimes they are larger offenses where we have been seriously sinned against. We have all been victims. Our life has been altered for the worse by the actions of another. It is quite normal to dwell on what happened, or even to dream of revengeful scenarios where the playing field will be level again. And yet, if we do not move swiftly from that vengeful state of mind, if we get stuck in our anger and bitterness—who suffers? We suffer. Our today and tomorrow is negatively affected and we end up in bondage to our own bitterness. When we don't forgive—when we don't seek God's power and grace to enable us to forgive—we suffer. We carry the hurt into the future. Bitterness takes root and poisons the rest of our lives, just as Lee pointed out.

The power of forgiveness is that it enables us to move forward, to live a life that is untangled by the past. Jesus wants us to have abundant life. Abundant life happens in part when we let go of the past.

Victims often become bitter, wishing only to get even. A crime victim said, "If you could lick my heart it would poison you." Forgiveness has the power to break the power of the past. When people say, "I can't forgive", what they really mean is "I won't forgive." One European author wrote a story about a man who borrowed some money and took two years to pay it back. The angry lender said to the man. "No keep the money—it's not worth changing my opinion of you." Forgiveness is not a feeling, but rather a clear choice, a conscious decision to use the power of grace to overcome the power of the past.

The first person who gains from forgiveness is the person who does the forgiving. There is a benefit to offering forgiveness. When we hold a grudge, we are often enslaved by our animosity towards others; forgiveness frees us and leads to emotional healing, even if there is no reconciliation. When we refuse to forgive, we become prison-

> The first person who gains from forgiveness is the person who does the forgiving.

ers of those who have hurt us. By forgiving, we let go of our resentment. The Hebrew word to forgive, "**Salach**", means "to have hatred in one's fist and to release it". The first thing we do in forgiving is to surrender our right to get even with the person who has wronged us. Forgiveness has the incredible power to stop the ongoing cycle of repaying vengeance with vengeance.

God's divine power is wrapped up in forgiveness. Many want to tap into God's healing and prosperity but do not want to let go of their past hurts. What you're looking for has been locked up in forgiveness. You may ask, "But what if I don't want to forgive? Does anything happen?" Yes, something does happen. Unforgiveness can be tragic because you will be unable to hold the key to healing and prosperity. The tragic consequences that may result can best be learned from this next story.

There was a merchant who had identical twin sons. The boys worked for their father in the department store he owned, and when he died, they took over the store. Everything went well until the day a dollar bill disappeared. One of the brothers had left the bill on the cash register and walked outside with a customer. When he returned, the money was gone. He asked his brother, "Did you see the dollar bill on the cash register?" His brother shook his head to say no, but the young man kept probing and questioning. He would not let up. "Dollar bills just don't get up and walk away! Surely you must have seen it!" There was a subtle accusation in the voice. Tempers began to rise. Resentment set in and before long, a deep and bitter chasm divided the young men. They refused to speak. They finally decided that they could no longer work together and a dividing wall was built down the center of the store. For twenty years hostility and bitterness grew, spreading to their families and to the community.

> The power of forgiveness can bring down every wall of resentments in your life.

Then one day a man drove to the store. He walked in and asked the clerk, "How long have you been here?" The clerk replied that he had been there all his life. The customer said, "I must share something with you. Twenty years ago, I was riding the rails and came into this town in a boxcar. I hadn't eaten for three days. I came into this store from the back door and saw a dollar bill on the cash register. I placed it in my pocket and walked out. All these years I haven't been able to forget that. I know it wasn't much money, but I had to come back and ask for your forgiveness."

The stranger was amazed to see tears well up in the eyes of this middle-age man. "Would you please go next door and tell that same story to the man in the store?" he said. Then the man was even more amazed to see two middle-aged men, who looked very much alike, embracing each other and weeping together in the front of the store. After twenty years, the disunion was mended. The wall of resentment that divided them had come down.

God has deposited a marvelous power in forgiveness. The power of forgiveness can bring down every wall of resentment in your life. That story may have sounded silly, but it actually happened. It is the little things that divide people. The solution, of course, is to let it go. There is really nothing particularly profound about it. For fulfilling and lasting relationships, letting past hurts go is a must. After you refuse to carry around bitterness and resentment, you may be surprised at how much energy you have left for building bonds with those you love. Another benefit of refusal will be the ability to tap into the grace of God available through forgiveness and lay hold on your healing and prosperity.

There is power embedded in forgiveness. You can access this power if you can just let it go. The absence of forgiveness in a person's life is a destructive bondage causing strife, division, depression, oppression, sickness, divorce, and even eternal damnation. You can break or pull down the walls of these hindering factors simply with the power of forgiveness.

Unforgiveness builds high walls of division, separation and alienation. But forgiveness has the power to change and heal the person forgiving and the one being forgiven, transforming them into better individuals.

Some years ago, two teenagers, with a long history of crime and delinquency, robbed a YMCA on the lowest Eastside of New York City. On the way out, they saw a young man at the telephone switchboard. They were frightened and assumed that he must be calling the police. They seized and beat him savagely with a brass knuckle and a car

> Unforgiveness builds high walls of division, separation and alienation.

jack. Assuming he was dead, they hid him behind a radiator near a swimming pool and escaped.

Later that evening, a woman who came to swim, was walking by the pool. She slipped in the man's blood, screamed, and then found Donald Tippet's body. He lived, but one eye was so badly damaged that it could not be saved. Meanwhile, the two teenagers were apprehended and brought to trial. Their past records assured that both would get long sentences. However, Donald Tippet did an amazing thing—he requested that the judge allow the two young men to be paroled to his charge. He wanted to give them another chance. He believed they could change.

One of the boys blew his opportunity, as he committed another crime, was caught and sent to jail. The other boy, however, was responsive to Tippet's kindness. He went to college and then eventually, to medical school. He became one of our nation's leading surgeons—an eye surgeon. One reporter, writing about Donald Tippet's amazing story of forgiveness, said of the surgeon's accomplishments. "I wonder if he ever performs one of these delicate eye operations without thinking of that night in the YMCA and the young man whose confidence and forgiveness changed his life!" Donald Tippet's heart of forgiveness gave opportunity for an eye surgeon to emanate from someone who should have been wasting in jail.

There is so much benefit for all when we tap into the power embedded in forgiveness. Forgiveness makes us a good soil for any of God's seeds. Tap into this power now!

"Father forgive them for they do not know what they do"…Lord Jesus Christ (Luke 23 v 34)

"I can forgive, but I cannot forget, is only another way of saying, I will not forgive. Forgiveness ought to be like a cancelled note—torn in two, and burned up, so that it can never be shown against one."—Henry Ward Beech

4

Forgive God?

We must look into asking God to forgive us for any anger, bitterness, or resentment we might have towards Him.

People become upset with God for a number of different reasons. Some might be upset with God because they feel He took a loved one they wished was still around. Some might be upset with God because they feel He will not cure their illness or that of a family member. Some might be upset with God because God will not grant them that job promotion they are seeking or feel they deserve. Others are upset with God because even after praying for the downfall of someone who has caused so much havoc in their lives, that person appears to advance and prosper. Many are very upset with God because in spite of their faithfulness, things in their life have not changed. Some are upset that God is too slow in helping them and doesn't move at their own fast pace. The list is endless.

Let me use this opportunity to tell you about my childhood friend Lt. Pere Brown, who should truly have had issues with God. We became friends when we were about ten years old. He went to Nigerian Military School in Zaria. After successfully completing his military secondary education, he proceeded to a cadet school called Nigeria Defense Academy in Kaduna, a city located in the northern part of Nigeria. He graduated at the top of his class and was commissioned into the Nigerian Navy as a Midshipman.

As a young naval officer, Pere was full of life, adventurous and had an enduring spirit. He served on many naval ships and shore assignments both in Nigeria and abroad. But on 17th December, 1982 at the age of 24, with a bright future ahead of him, he had a fatal car accident with his then brand new Toyota Celica. The accident occurred in the weary hours of the morning while returning to his naval base after a year end party. He fell asleep while driving and his car skidded off the rails on one of the bridges in Lagos and crashed onto the ground below. It was indeed a miracle that he survived the accident. The car was wrecked beyond repairs. Pere was rushed to the hospital where the doctors confirmed our worst fear, that he had sustained a spinal cord injury.

The Nigeria Navy did their best for this then young naval officer by sending him to London, England for further medical treatment. After spending a year in treatment and rehabilitation in London, he returned to Nigeria to spend the remainder of his life in a bed and a wheel chair.

Pere had every reason to be upset with God. He was kind, loved every one that he got to meet and know. He asked God several times why me? I am sure Christopher Reeves, who played the character "Superman" in a U.S. television program a few years back and so many others who have experienced such horrific and unexpected injury of this magnitude, have asked the same question. We must all realize that God is our Creator, He can not be questioned. Certain things that happens to us, though it may seem unfair, most often it is for our own good and for the betterment of the society at large, as you will find here in Pere's continuous story.

I can attest to this because I saw God used Pere to do mighty things. God enlarged his coast by giving him a restive spirit and as result he was not bound by that wheel chair or his bed. After being retired from the Navy on medical grounds he was given a political appointment as the officer in charge of Naval Officers Wives Association (NOWA) welfare centre Lagos which was used to train naval rating personals. To perform his then new job to the best of his ability, he resorted to mastering the computer and internet. He became a "wizard" in countless number of computer software and the network technology which enabled him to train not only the naval ratings under his stewardship but others that have dropped out of school or could not find jobs. God used Pere to touch the lives of many people, he probably would not have but for the accident. Pere went to be with the Lord during the final phase of this book, after solid twenty four years of great achievements despite being on the wheel chair. During Pere's burial, I was moved yet again when another person in a wheel chair testified how God used Pere to save his life as he had made final preparation to commit suicide a few years back.

Also a few years ago, my dear cousin, Mary, went to be with the Lord. She was indeed a God-fearing woman, she went to Church weekly prayed daily, fasted, was married with four children. Everything about Mary was her dedication and love for Jesus Christ.

After she was diagnosed with Leukemia, her prayer group in which she was the President, prayed and fasted for healing, but it did not happen. Mary's children needed her, her husband needed her, and we all needed her. But guess who needed her the most, God. None of us have control over when we came to this world, nor when we exit. God has supreme control.

> None of us have control over when we came to this world, nor when we exit. God has Supreme control.

In the book of Ecclesiastes Chapter 3 verses 1-2, said:

> "To everything there is a season, and a
> time to every purpose under the heaven, a time
> to be born and a time to die."

So if you had someone taken away from you, who you felt was too young or was too needed to go, and it made you resentful toward God, ask God for His forgiveness.

The book of Isaiah Chapter 55 verses 8-9 said;

> "For my thoughts are not your thoughts,
> neither your ways are my ways, says the Lord.

> For as the heaven is higher than the earth,
> so are my ways higher than your ways and
> my thoughts than your thoughts."

I do not know which areas of life you may be upset, resentful or angry with God. Bear in mind that his thoughts towards you are for good and not evil, to give you hope and a future. In the book of Romans chapter 8 verse 28; we were assured that all things are working for our own good as eluded to earlier on. You do not need to be resentful towards God. Go back to him now and ask for forgiveness and ask Him what He wants you to learn from what you might perceive to be a predicament. God will then show how He intends to use whatever situation we find ourselves for His glory. Always bear in mind that it is all about God.

> Always bear in mind that it is all about God.

I will like to end this chapter with a beautiful quote from the book of Numbers chapter 23 verse 19 and I want you to think about it.

> "God is not a man that he should lie,
> nor a son of man that He should repent.
> Has he said something and will not do it?
> Has he promised something and not fulfilled it?"

"If you forgive others their wrongs, your father in heaven will also forgive yours. If you do not forgive others then your father in heaven will not forgive you either...Lord Jesus Christ (Matthew 6 v14)

"A wise man will make haste to forgive, because He knows the true value of time, and will not like to suffer and indulge in an unnecessary pain."—Samuel Johnson

5

Forgive Yourself

Many of us may be troubled by horrible things we have done in the past. Some have been prostitutes, murderers, abortionist, womanizers, sugar mommies or daddies; the list goes on and on. Today, we have given up most of those bad tendencies to become better people. Nevertheless, the past still replays itself to us each time we pray or sit to meditate.

John Piper said, "Until we fear sin and its consequences more keenly, we will not prize our pardon very highly". Although many of us prize our pardon highly, we still have a problem completely forgiving ourselves even when God has forgiven us. Our confession of sins is more than merely informing God that we have sinned. It also involves a turning away. We therefore need to turn our hearts away from thinking or punishing ourselves further for sins that God has already forgiven us for.

Stop dragging your forgiven sins along, forgive yourself and enjoy the freedom God has given. In this award winning film called "The Mission," Robert DeNiro Plays a mercenary who has taken asylum in the local church after killing his brother in a pit of jealous rage. He eventually leaves the church and heads to a mission post located above the waterfalls in a South American jungle. Due to his past actions, and the deep remorse he feels, he ties himself to several hundred pounds of items, which represent his sinful life. He feels compelled to drag this sack of sin with him as a way of penance for what he has done.

> Stop dragging your forgiven sins along.

27

If you watch this clip, you will see him slip under the burden of his past while the rope chokes the very life out of him. He is overcome with guilt and continues to struggle with the accompanying sin and shame. Have you ever felt like that? I suspect that you might be tethered to some transgression in your life while others might be gasping under the guilt of something they did several years ago. What do you do when you realize you have messed up? How do you stabilize your life when you experience more ups and downs than the stock market? Where do you go when you have failed? Where do you turn when you have hurt those closest to you? Do you grab a rope, hitch it up to your sin pile and start dragging? Or, is there something better?

Many drag around nets of iniquity for a long time. I've done the same thing before now…and so have you. Many in the church today are carrying boat loads of bitterness and truck loads of trespasses. The only way to dispose of your regrets and put the past behind, is to confess them to God. When you do, he will forgive you. And when he does, your sins will be forgotten and you will be free! Some have asked for forgiveness but still pull a suitcase of sin along with them. A good practice for those who belong to the catholic faith is to confess their sins to their local Priest.

There is another scene in "The Mission" where Robert DeNiro was struggling with his load of guilt and someone cuts the rope. His net of iniquity goes tumbling down the path and into the water. Instead of being thankful, DeNiro pushes the man out of the way and runs after his sins. When he

> God not only covers our sins, He turns us into a new person.

gets down to the water, he picks up the bundle again and tries to carry it back up the mountain on his back.

Are you doing the same thing today? If you have confessed and repented, God has forgiven you. Can you forgive yourself? You see, the only way for God to glorify His name and make people happy is not just to overlook sins, but also to change sinners. God not only covers our sins, He turns us into a new person. This was clearly stated in the book of 2nd Corinthians chapter 5 verse 17 when it said:

> "Therefore, if anyone is in Christ, he is
> a new creature: old things are passed
> away: behold all things have become new"

Enjoy this newness and stop carrying over the old.

One young girl, Jodi Kosan, experienced the same thing. She always asked herself, "Why do I feel empty inside and a sense of guilt?" She came from a good Christian family. She tried smoking and drinking to appear cool to her peers. She become sexually active at a very young age, and that only brought more despair, guilt and heartache. She experimented with Ouijaa Board, read horoscopes, and watched many horror movies that left scars of fear in her life for years to come. Her interest in dark music grew and she often had thoughts of suicide. She had many boyfriends and found herself in a relationship far too serious for a girl of her age.

At fifteen, she was pregnant and was faced with the horrific question of keeping or terminating the pregnancy. A nurse tried to reassure her by telling her that the fetus wasn't really a human until it took its first breathe of air. (She realizes now that was lie, but the façade helped her justify her actions at the time). After a week of deep thoughts and despair, she made a painful decision. She was terrified of losing her boyfriend, her friends, her "so called freedom", and being shunned by the community. She put her needs ahead of the baby. She decided to terminate the pregnancy. She still felt she was living in deep darkness and became extremely depressed. She felt lost, alone, afraid, scared, and tormented by her irretrievable choice.

Her parents did not know about her abortion until eight years later. She said, "If there is a God, he must hate me even more now. He could not possibly forgive me for what I had done." Before graduating from high school, she met her future husband in Winnipeg. In 1990, she got married to Tim. She figured she would become whole after marriage, but after only her second year of wedlock, she found herself lonely again. One night, due to immense feelings of guilt, she struggled to fall asleep. She was tired of being afraid and feeling so all alone in her pain. It continued for a while until she joined a mother's help group at a nearby church. It was in that group that she met some wonderful women who made her re-evaluate her life. She noticed that the women had something she lacked.

> Guilt damages our relationships, when we live without forgiving ourselves, we respond to people in wrong ways.

Not riches, gold, fame or fortune, but a gentle peace of mind she could not explain. She opened up to them about family issues and personal hurts. They prayed for her, asked her to receive the Lord Jesus Christ, and to forgive herself. She realized that she no longer had to feel guilty and anguish over the choices she made as an adolescent, because Jesus has forgiven her.

What about you? Do you regret the choices you've made? Do you have guilt and pain hidden in your heart as you read this book? It doesn't have to be that way; forgive yourself just as Jesus has forgiven you. He does not keep records of your past, so stop keeping these records and hurting yourself. Release yourself today and enjoy the grace he has made available to you by going to the cross.

Before we go over to the next part, let's take a look at a few effects of guilt as described by Jeff Seaman on sermoncentral.com:

> Guilt destroys our confidence. Guilt can make us feel insecure because we are always worried that someone is going to find out what we were really like, or what we've really done. Many years ago, Sir Arthur Conan Doyle, the Author of the Sherlock Holmes, novels played a prank on five of the most prominent men in England. He sent an anonymous note to each one that simply said this, "All is found out, flee at once." Within 24 hours all five men had left the country. The above situation was best described in the book of Proverbs chapter 28 verse 1 when it said:
>
> > "The wicked man flees even when

no one is after him but the virtuous
man feels as safe as a lion."

Guilt damages our relationships, when we live without forgiving ourselves, we respond to people in wrong ways. Are you rather impatient
with others? Do you find yourself reacting unnecessarily in anger?
Are you pulling back from those you love? If so, there may be some
guilt in your guts somewhere.

Guilt keeps us stuck in the past. Do you continuously replay your
sins over and over in your mind? Someone has said, "Guilt cannot
change the past just like worry cannot change the future. But it can
make you miserable always.

It is time to lay aside every weight of guilt, forgive your self, and live free.
Drop the loads today and move on! A recommended prayer for asking of forgiveness from God is the same prayer King David
prayed to God after being confronted by Prophet
Nathan over his affairs with Bath-Sheba which is
Psalm 51. Special attention should be placed on
verses 1-2, 7 and 10-12.

> Guilt keeps us stuck
> in the past.

"Have mercy upon me, O God according to
thy loving kindness: according to thy multitude
of tender mercies blot out my transgressions.
Wash me thoroughly and cleanse me from my sin.
Purge me with hyssop, and I shall be clean; wash me
and I shall be whiter than snow. Create in me a clean heart,
O God and renew a right spirit within me. Cast me not away
from your presence and take not thy holy Spirit away
from me. Restore unto me thy joy of thy salvation
and uphold me with thy free spirit."—In the name of
Our Jesus Christ I pray—amen, amen.

"If your brother or sister has sinned against you, go and point out the fault when two of you are in private, and if he listens to you, you have won your brother or sister. If you are not listened to, take with you one or two others so that the case may be decided by the evidence of two or three witness"...Lord Jesus Christ (Matthew 18 v 15-16)

"In the long run, it's not a question of whether they deserve to be forgiven. You're not forgiving them for their sake. You're doing it for yourself. For your own health and well being, forgiveness is simply the most energy-efficient option. It frees you from the incredibly toxic, debilitating drain of holding a grudge. Don't let these people live rent free in your head. If they hurt you before, why let them keep doing it year after year in your mind. You can muster that heart power to forgive them as a way of looking out for yourself. It's one thing you can be totally selfish about."—Childre and Howard Martin

6

Forgive Others and Steps to Reconciliation

We must learn to forgive one another. There are situations when those who have sinned against us believe they have done nothing wrong or that their actions were justified. The Lord gave us a great idea on how to handle these situations in Matthew chapter 18 verse 15. Let explore the Lord's statement again—

> "If your brother or sister has sinned
> against you, go and point out the fault
> when you are in private, and if he listens
> to you, you have won your brother."

Make the first move

It is important you discuss the issue or sin with God. Pray about the conflict instead of telling all your friends about it and before discussing it with your alleged offender. Most often you will discover that the Lord can easily change your heart or the heart of your offender.

> It is important you discuss the issue or sin with God.

Cry to God about your frustrations. Tell Him how upset and exasperated you are. God is not surprised about any of your emotions. He is your creator and he built those emotions there in the first place.

To the Lord it does not matter who was at fault. As Christians, we are expected to make the first move in contacting our alleged offender after the appropriate prayer to God. You must not procrastinate or make excuses. The Lord is commanding us here to immediately schedule a meeting with the one we have conflict with. When you delay scheduling the meeting, it will only increase your bitterness and resentment, just as your enemy the devil prescribes. The bible teaches us to resist the devil and he will flee from us. Do not worry about the offender rejecting your move, do it anyway.

The Lord advises us to have this meeting in private. A private meeting will help enhance the successful possibility of the scheduled talk. It is not a good idea to schedule such a meeting when both parties are tired, rushed or might be interrupted. It must be in a peaceful atmosphere.

> Do not worry about the offender rejecting your move, do it anyway.

Listen to one another

Listening is instrumental when attempting to solve any disagreement. You should use your ears more than your mouth. You should sympathize with each other's feelings. Look out for each other's interest. The primary focus should be on the offender feelings, not your own.

Do not at any time attempt to ridicule your offender about their feelings. Do the listening and let them unload whatever is on their mind. Give nodding gestures that you do understand even when you do not necessarily agree with their position.

When you listen, you are in effect telling them that "You and this relationship are important to me, you matter a whole lot and I love you". It is not easy to absorb the unfounded anger of others. But we must do this because the Word commanded us to do so as was clearly voiced in the book of James chapter 1 verse 19:

"My beloved be quick to hear
but slow to speak and slow to anger,
For human anger does not fulfill the
justice of God."

Take responsibility for your part in the problem

Prior to the scheduled meeting, pray and ask God to reveal to you whatever mistakes you made in the conflict and take complete responsibility for your role. Admit your mistakes or sin to the one you are having the conflict with. Jesus said in the book of Matthew chapter 7 verses 3-5:

"Why do you look at the log in your
brother's eye and not see the log in your
own eye? How can you say to your brother
come let me take the speck from your eye, as
long as there is a log in your own? Hypocrite, take first the
log of your own eye, then you see clear enough to take
the log out of your brother's eye."

So pray earnestly and the Lord will show you where you were at fault. Confessing your part in the conflict is great tool for reconciliation. By humbly admitting your mistakes it will not only melt down their anger it will also disarm them from attacking you. You must honestly own up to any role or part you played in the conflict. Ask for forgiveness and own up to your mistakes.

Make the conflict the issue and work on reconciliation

Problems can not be resolved if you are consumed with who is to be blamed. Not too long ago, some high school students ruined a project in which I was responsible. I was upset when I confronted them, not realizing that the tone of my voice and remarks were rather inflammatory. One of the young men told me rather politely that I should calm down

> How you say something is just as important as what you say.

and they will fix the problem. I apologized for the tone of my voice and remarks and immediately sought their forgiveness. And like that, the situation was resolved.

The point is that it is difficult for you to get across to people if you can not control your own emotions. How you say something is just as important as what you say. If you come across respectively, you will often receive a positive response. If you come across disrespectively, you will more than likely receive a negative response. If you are abrasive you can hardly be persuasive.

As a God fearing person, you should do everything within your power to eliminate inflammatory remarks, which include being sarcastic, belittling, judgmental, condescending, comparing and insulting. You must stay focus on the issue and use reconciliatory remarks such as, "I am sorry", "It was not my intention", "It was a honest mistake", "You and this relationship means so much to me", "You are the best in what you do", or "God loves you and so do I". These outlined steps, in most cases, should help resolve some conflicts and lead to reconciliation.

Get respected people involved;

The Lord realizes there might be cases where you need to involve someone else to help you resolve your conflicts, as evidenced in the verse 16 of the book of Matthew chapter 18 when He said;

> "If you are not listened to, take with you
> one or two others so that the case may be
> decided by the evidence of two or three witnesses."

The person should be a close relative or someone that you both respect highly. A person that both of you would listen to. Your local Pastor is highly recommended. If you are not comfortable with your Pastor, you might want to use the services of a professional counselor. If these efforts fail and they still do not bulge, then

> If you are abrasive you can hardly be persuasive.

leave it in the hands of God. Let God know in your prayers that you have done everything in your power and you are now handing over the matter to him. Now, simply watch God take over.

"And forgive us our sins as we forgive those who do us wrong. And lead us not into temptation, but deliver us from evil"...Lord Jesus Christ (Luke 11 v 4)

"Strength of character means the ability to overcome resentment against hurt feelings, and to forgive quickly."—Lawrence G. Lovasik.

7

The Most Important Prayer

You might be wondering why this is the most important prayer, not only is it the most detailed prayer in the bible, but it also places a strong emphasis on forgiveness. When was the last time you said the Lord's Prayer? You must include the Lord's Prayer in your daily devotion and in your Saturday or Sunday services if you are not already doing so. You should also expect this prayer to be prayed during conventions. The Lord's Prayer should and must be the heavenly anthem for Christians all over the world. This is the prayer that our Lord Jesus Christ himself taught us to say. It is rather most disheartening that all year long, most churches do not say the Lord's Prayer during their services.

> The Lord's Prayer should and must be the heavenly anthem for Christians all over the world.

But in most instances we go to different sporting events like, football, soccer, or baseball games, usually before the kick offs, we all stand and sing our national anthem as a sign of patriotism and respect to our countries, and there's nothing wrong with that.

In early 2004, in Tunis, Tunisia in Africa, during the African Nations Cup, before the semi-final soccer game between the host country Tunisia and Nigeria, the host country did not play the Nigerian national anthem right before the game began. So before the second half began the Nigeria delegate made the host country replay their national anthem before they could resume play. This is an example of how much value we place on the national anthem. It shows pride, respect, and patriotism to our individual countries. If you do not get anything from this message but bring this Lord's Prayer issue to the forefront of your church, you would have done a great service for God.

Let's reinstate the Lord's Prayer in its entirety again. It is found in the book of **Luke 11 v 1-4** and in **Matthew 6 v 9-13**

"And it came to pass, that as He was praying in a Certain place, when He ceased, one of His disciples said unto Him, Lord teach us to pray as John taught his disciples. And He said unto them, when you pray, say;

Our Father who art in heaven, Hallowed be thy name, May thy kingdom come, May thy will be done on earth as it is in heaven. Give us this day our daily bread. And forgive us our sins as we forgive every one that have sinned against us. And lead us not into temptation but deliver us from evil.

The book of Matthew 6 v 13 added; for thine is the kingdom, the power and glory for ever and ever.

The point of our discussion is on one particular verse. In Luke, chapter 11, verse 4, and Matthew chapter 6, verse 12,

"Forgive us our sins, as we forgive those who are indebted to us."

There is a condition to be met here. This implies that in order for any of us to ask and receive God's favor, which includes the forgiveness of our sins, we must already have forgiven our friends, relations, enemies, brothers, sisters and even our parents. The book of Matthew, chapter 6, verse 14, the Amplified Version said it best, "If you forgive others their wrongs, your Father in heaven will forgive yours." If you don't forgive others, then your father will not forgive you either.

In order to get the spiritual growth, healing and prosperity you desire, you must forgive and restore the relationship with the one that has offended you. This must be done prior to asking God for forgiveness. Most of the teachings of Jesus Christ center on love and forgiveness.

In Matthew chapter 5, verse 23, Jesus said:

"So then, if you are about to offer your gift at the altar, and you remember that your brother has sinned against you, Leave your gift there in front of the altar, go at once and make peace with him, and then come back and offer your gift."

It is simply saying that if you do not have forgiveness in your heart, there is no need giving to any ministry or church. You are simply planting your seed on bad soil. If you are reading this right now, and you have someone that has done you wrong, you need to give them a call or send them a letter, letting them know you have forgiven them, and that you wish to restore your relationship with them. Only then you can be assured that any seed you sow will bring about a great harvest of blessings and treasure in the Lord.

Some Christians go to church, and sit close to someone that they perceive to be their enemy, or someone that has offended them. Some change their

> You cannot keep carrying all these grudges and still expect God to give you a bountiful harvest or healing.

seats. Some sit there but put on a long face. They still sing praises, pray and worship, but refuse to speak to this person, and yet they feel they are serving God. Do not allow the enemy to deceive you, you have no doubt been going to church, but the truth is that you have not been serving God. Some of us cannot pick up the phone and call our moms, dads, brothers, sisters, cousins, nephews or nieces because of whatever sins we feel they have committed against us. But I want to tell you that you cannot keep carrying all these grudges and still expect God to give you a bountiful harvest or healing. Do not give the enemy the opportunity to hinder your spiritual progress and steal your healing, prosperity and chance of establishing a glorious relationship with your God.

Many find it difficult to forgive because they may have been sexually assaulted by a familiar face. They continue to nurse this hurtful feeling deep in their heart. Some were probably a victim of incest like the woman of God, Joyce Meyer. Joyce Meyer is preaching today freely from her heart. As an incest victim, she nursed painful feelings for a long while, until God touched her to LET IT GO! Some years back, she baptized her father after he gave his life completely to the service of God. If Joyce Meyer could forgive her father, you can too. Make up your mind today to let it go.

Maybe you were probably cheated on by your spouse or your spouse walked out on you. Dave experienced this kind of heart break from his wife whom he loved dearly. He felt that his wife was a perfect match and after a few years of marriage they had a son and daughter who were multiple blessings from God.

Dave was a boilermaker, working in the deep goldmines of South Africa. Dave's work entailed heavy steelwork maintenance and the handing of dangerous chemicals such as caustic soda and cyanide, which was used in the process of extracting the gold out of the ore. Most of the other artisans were afraid to work with these chemicals, but Dave felt he was well-trained in the proper safety precautions, and boldly accepted the daunting tasks. Dave prided himself to the fact that he could do any job better and faster than any other artisan, and no job was too big or too small. He would tackle any job or challenge with great enthusiasm. He not only had to be the best artisan, but he also had to do the best in all fields of his work. At the end of the day, he would return home to his family thoroughly exhausted from the day's work.

At this time in his life, Dave was not a Christian but his wife was totally committed to Christ. Dave would occasionally go with her to church out of duty to his children and his wife. While sitting in church, he would count the minutes until the service was over, as he did not completely embrace God as his wife said he could. Dave and his wife slowly started to grow apart and the more his wife got involved with the Church, the more Dave became engrossed in his own work. So much so, that Dave's work became first in his life and everything else became second, including his family.

Suddenly, the gold price on the world markets fell to all time low, causing mines to retrench employees and close certain sections of the mines, as they could not afford to keep them running any longer. In an effort to get better job security, Dave decided to interview for a job at a cement factory about 150 kilometers from the gold mine he was currently working. He was offered and accepted the job without hesitation, and without considering his wife's feelings about moving. Dave's wife had been born and raised in the same town. Her entire life, including her friends, church, and family were in this same town.

Nevertheless, they moved and Dave started the process of becoming the best worker at his new job. Dave was so involved in this new work that he didn't even notice the deep depression his wife began to experience. He was far more concerned with what was happening in his own life to take any concern about his wife. He did continue to provide for his family the best he knew how, well so he thought. Throughout this time, his wife never stopped praying for Dave to become a Christian and she had the faith in God that it would someday come to pass. Dave attended the local church, but only because his wife did not know anyone and she felt insecure on her own. After a few months, Dave started skipping church and eventually stopped going altogether. During this period, his wife fell deeper and deeper into depression. She began to see the pastor for counseling and they started a relationship as friends. He became her comforter as she could talk to him about the Lord, unlike her husband.

One day, while at work, Dave received an anonymous letter. It was strange for him to get a letter at work because he had a post box and all his mail was sent there. He opened the letter and it read as follows: *DO YOU KNOW ABOUT YOUR WIFE'S AFFAIR?* That was the day Dave's life fell apart. Dave had grown up in a divorced home and the first thing that came into his mind was that history was about to repeat itself for his own children. All that day at work, Dave wrestled with the contents of the letter, he didn't know for a fact if the letter was a prank or not. He was totally unable to work or communicate with anyone. Dave went to his boss and asked for a few days off due to a family emergency.

When Dave got home, his wife immediately knew something was wrong, as his current facial expression was unbeknownst to her. Dave told the children to get their swimming costumes and go swim at the recreation club swimming pool for the remainder of the afternoon. Dave showed his wife the letter and demanded an explanation, desperately trying to hold onto his last ounce of sanity. Dave started to recall his past and how he had immigrated to South Africa from Zimbabwe. He was involved in a terrible civil war where he did two years mandatory service in the South African

> In a state of total brokenness, the Lord had come to him.

defensive force. He once thought that if he could get out of the war alive after seeing what men are capable of doing to each other, then he would survive anything the world could throw at him. He never considered his present predicament. He snaps back as his wife confesses to the affair and names the pastor of their church as the accomplice. It had been going on for some months.

Obviously, Dave was devastated; he didn't even see this coming. After much discussion, confused and angered, Dave went outside to face the dark night only to be overcome by an unrecognizable feeling. He later realized it was the Holy Spirit that had come over him. In a state of total brokenness, the Lord had come to him. He spent the next few hours on a roller coaster of emotions, from deep depression to an intense joy. Dave thought this to be somewhat extreme and could not quite comprehend its meaning. Dave gave his life to the Lord that night and pleaded with the Lord to forgive and help him. He also asked his wife for forgiveness and at the same time forgave her.

The following morning (neither Dave nor his wife had slept), Dave realized that he had not been the ideal husband and admitted his failure to his wife. Although he was deeply hurt, he realized that he still loved his wife and he didn't want to be separated from his children. Dave phoned the Pastor and told him to come to his house. The pastor arrived and Dave sat everyone down. He asked his wife to make a decision to stay with him or to go with the Pastor. Dave's wife decided to stay with him. The pastor then said that his life and his ministry were over and he would have no alternative but to kill himself. Dave immediately told the pastor that as an adult he was responsible for his own actions and whatever he did was his own responsibility. He then told the pastor to leave and that he was no longer welcome in Dave's house.

Needless to say, the pastor was transferred to another church. Dave's wife stood up in front of the entire congregation, and disregarding all consequences, confessed her sin and asked for forgiveness. This act was a risk she chose to bear, she could have been totally rejected from the congregation or they could have seen her true remorse and how contrite she was for allowing the affair to have happened. This is a true step of courage and faith. Some people would rather move to another church than face judgment from others. Yes, there were people who condemned her, even to this day, but Dave's wife knows that she did the right thing before God and the Church. She spent many months learning how to cope with the stigma some people placed over her, but Dave and God were always there to support her.

Dave was asked one day as to why he did not do anything to stop the pastor from preaching further and to get him out of church altogether. Dave replied with the following; "At the time of my need before God I asked him to forgive me for all that I had done in my life. How could I expect God to forgive me and then not forgive the Pastor? The other reason is if God can still use the Pastor to save just one more soul for Him, isn't that more important than my own life or the guilt and shame that I will have to carry with me for the rest of my life. Judgment is not for me but for God, the Pastor will have to ask God for forgiveness for what he has done. As for me, I've forgiven him and if God forgives him then it must be so. Although the pain from going through such an ordeal does not just go away easily, I have learned how to truly forgive. I have forgiven my wife, my Pastor and myself." Forgiving someone is indeed a difficult thing for anyone to do, but remember this one thing; if you cannot forgive someone for what they have done to you, how then can God forgive you for your sins? And we are all sinful.

Dave and his wife are living quite an extraordinary life now. They are involved in the church, Sunday school, Emmaus movement, and the Kairos prison ministry for maximum security prisoners. Dave got a new job in the same cement factory, which has much better working conditions and a higher salary. I am sharing this story of Dave and his wife because situations like this are not often brought into the open within our churches. If you have been in a similar situation and can relate to this story, I pray that this story will give you the courage to do it God's way; forgive all who have hurt you, especially if the culprit is your spouse.

Maybe someone killed or caused the death of a loved one. Since then, you have been dragging along loads of resentment and hurtful feelings. It is time to drop these loads, making you lighter and enabling you to move at the required pace or speed and get all God has in store for you.

Michael McGoldrick and his wife turned on their TV and heard that a taxi driver had been murdered. They didn't think it could be anyone close to them or else they would have already heard. But the news report continued, "Taxi driver, married with one child, wife expecting another baby…" Michael's wife, Bridie, looked at him in cold denial. Then the next sentence came, "He just graduated from University on Friday." It was their son. They rushed out through the front door of their house. Michael hit the ground on his knees and in desperation started pounding his fists. He looked up and cried, "Hanging on a cross is nothing compared to what we are going through!" The he looked at his wife and said, "We'll never smile again."

The next day, Michael and his wife made the decision to take their own lives. Their son was everything they had. Bridie suffered from arthritis, and so they had plenty of tablets. As Michael went out to the Kitchen, suddenly a picture of the crucified Christ came into his mind. It hit him that God's son had also been murdered. He knew that what they planned to do was wrong. It amazed him how God intervened in such a miraculous way in order to sway their minds. Before he closed his son's coffin, he laid his hand upon him and said, "Goodbye, son, I'll see you in heaven." At that very moment, he experienced the power of God flowing through his body.

He was filled with a great sense of joy and confidence in God. He felt as if he could have faced Goliath—he never felt as strong in his whole life.

During the funeral, he wrote on the back of an envelope a word which came to him so calm and lucid, referring to those who had murdered his son; "Bury your pride with my son." At the bottom he wrote, "Forgive them." He felt that, despite the agony they were going through, God had given him a message of peace, forgiveness and reconciliation. He spoke that message in front of the TV cameras that morning and stands by it to this day. He said, "The power and grace I experienced to forgive from my heart was such a freedom and release. I know that resentment and bitterness would have killed me. After my son's murder, God gave me a clear grasp of the horror of sin, and I remember saying to God; 'These hands will never do any evil again.' I realized that in the same way I have offered forgiveness to those who killed my son; God has forgiven me my sins." Every morning he asks God to continue to give him the grace to forgive those who murdered his son.

Sometimes it is impossible for us to solely carry the burden of grief thrust upon us. We have to give it up and I have discovered that the best thing to do is to give it to God. He takes it completely off your shoulders and points you in a different direction.

Since his son's death, Michael became a changed man. Along with Bridie, he has started a relief ministry to orphanages in Romania. He feels as if Christ has taken hold of his life and he now wants to take hold of Christ by giving his life to God and by serving people.

There are millions of people right now that are unable to get out of their beds because they are suffering from one kind of sickness or the other, and they continually pray for healing. Many are on these beds because of one thing or the other that is chewing them up in the inside. A researcher at the University of Michigan's School of Public Health, found that people who forgive easily tend to enjoy greater psychological well-being and have less depression that those who hold grudges. Many are on these sick beds expecting to get better through the prescribed drugs, while others expect divine healing from God. They can make their case and their well-being much better if they can release and let go of all resentments and all forms of bitterness in their hearts, but if they have unforgiveness they probably will not experience complete healing. Some people have been healed, but due to the state of their heart, or their lingering unforgiveness, the sickness returned. We must forgive so that we can completely be healed.

"…The son will not be he held responsible for the sin of his father and the father will not be responsible for the sin of his son…" Prophet Ezekiel (Ezekiel 18 v 20)

"Beginnings today, treat everyone you meet as if they were going to be dead by midnight. Extend to them all the care, kindness, and understanding you can muster, and do it with no thought of any reward. Your life will never be the same again".—Og Mandina

8

Forgiving a Past Generation

Simon Wiesenthal lost eighty nine relatives in Hitler's death camps. He has devoted his life to finding Nazi criminals and bringing them to justice. He is often asked when he will give up. After all, he is hunting down men in their 70's and 80's for crimes committed half a century ago.

Wiesenthal answered by writing a book. The book begins with a true experience he had while he himself was a concentration camp prisoner. One day he was yanked out of a work, arrested and taken up a back stairway to a dark hospital room. A nurse let him into the room then left him alone with a figure wrapped in white, lying on a bed. The man was a badly wounded German soldier whose entire face was covered with bandages. His name was Karl.

With a trembling voice, the German made a sort of confession to Wiesenthal. He told how he had been brought up in a Nazi family, the fighting he had experienced on the Russian front, and the brutal measures his S. S. unit had taken against Jews. He then told him of a terrible atrocity. All the Jews in a town were moved into a wooden building that was then set on fire. Karl had taken an active part in the crime. Several times Wiesenthal tried to leave the room, but each time the ghost like figure reached out and begged him to stay. Finally, after two hours, Karl told Wiesenthal why he had been summoned.

The soldier had asked a nurse if any Jews still existed. If so he wanted one brought to his room so he could clear his conscience. He then said to

Wiesenthal—"I am left here with my guilt. I do not know who you are, I know only that you are a Jew and that's enough. I know that what I am asking is almost too much for you but without your answer I cannot die in peace." Karl asked for forgiveness for all the Jews he had killed. He asked forgiveness from a man who might soon die. Wiesenthal sat in silence for some time. He stared at the man's bandage face. At last, without saying a word, he stood up and left the room. He left the dying soldier in torment, and with an unforgiving soul.

Had Simon Wiesenthal done the best he could? He seemed dissatisfied with his own action. He went over this event with many of his companions. He visited the dead soldier's mother. In his book, he asks thirty two Rabbis, Christian theologians, and secular philosophers to comment. "What would you have done?" is the question he posed. Out of the thirty two people he asked the majority said he had done right in leaving the soldier unforgiving. Only six said he had done wrong. In my opinion Simon should have offered forgiveness, a true Christian would. When Jesus died on the cross, as most of us know, he was nailed to the cross in the company of two other known criminals, but one of them gave his life to him. Jesus Christ told him "Today you will be with me in Paradise." Think and reflect on the terrible cost of the refusal to forgive. Remember if you are saved today it is only because you yourself have been forgiven as I have just indicated. Don't make the same mistake as Simon Wiesenthal, instead, release and let go of all hostile feelings you have towards anyone, even if they have killed someone dear to you.

Ravensbruck was a concentration camp built in 1939 on a small lake opposite the city of Fuurstenberg, fifty six miles north of Berlin, Germany. It was built for women most of whom were part of the resistance to Nazi occupation.

The Ravensbruck women were an active part of the Dutch and French Resistance movement. They were among the first to be taken prisoners by the Nazis. They are of special importance because of the collective courage of these individuals, which united them against fascism and racism. Over ninety thousand women and children perished in Ravensbruck and little, if anything is written about them in modern history books. But we have learned at least one thing from Ravensbruck. It was written on a tattered, ripped and worn sheet of paper. It was found in the clothing of a dead child at Ravensbruck. It read, "O Lord, remember not only the men and women of good will, but also those of ill will. But do not remember all of the suffering they have inflicted upon us." Let us all learn from this said note and let go and forgive the sins of generations before us and don't hold their offsprings responsible for the sins of their fathers.

You might say, "But isn't God's grace and forgiveness free? Aren't you asking us to earn our salvation by forgiving those who harm us?" The answer is, yes, God's grace is free, but it is not cheap. When God's grace comes into our lives, it does not leave us as we were, it changes us. And one of the first changes that it makes is to empower us to forgive. By forgiving others, we are proving that we accept God's forgiveness, and are living within it. If we refuse to forgive those who harm us, we are showing that we do not really accept God's grace, and thus it is removed from us.

There is a lot of mental and emotional work involved in forgiving someone or a past generational sin. If you have ever tried to forgive someone that has truly offended you, you understand the difficulty. There is a serious price to pay when the choice is made to forgive a person. Sometimes, we can get used to being angry with a person or with people of past generation that we become so entranced that it seems like nothing else in life matters. We feed off that anger. So when we forgive, when we release that focused anger, our psychological order is altered. Without that anger to mesmerize us, we may become lost and helpless people. The on going bitter feud in the Middle East today is a great case in point.

To forgive means to say, "What you have said or done was truly and deeply hurtful to me, and though I feel the pain of what you have done, I choose to release you. You have earned and deserve my anger but instead I release you from your guilt." The above statement is easier said than done. Most people refrain because to them, the cost is too high. It's been said that true forgiveness is hard to extend because it demands that people let go of something that they value, such as pride, justice or revenge. When we forgive others it is evident that we acknowledge just how much God has forgiven us.

A Sunday school teacher had just concluded her lesson and wanted to make sure she had made her point. She said, "Can anyone tell me what needs to be done to obtain forgiveness of sin." There was a short pause and then, from the back of the room, a little boy spoke up. "Sin," he said.

Humans have a lot in common. With our world at war it seems like all we have in common are our differences. We all need to eat. We all need shelter and clothing. We all need to give and receive love. We all sin and need forgiveness.

The problem is that many of us are not sincerely ready to forgive or be forgiven. Rabbi David A. Nelson likes to tell the story of two brothers who went to their rabbi to settle a long-standing feud. The Rabbi got the two to reconcile their differences and shake hands. As they were about to leave, he asked each one to make a wish for the other in honor of the Jewish New Year. The first brother turned to the other and said. "I wish you what you wish me." At that, the second brother threw up his hand and said "See, Rabbi, he's starting up again!" It is very true then that many promising reconciliation attempts have broken down because while both parties come prepared to forgive, neither party come prepared to be forgiven. Stop for a moment and just think about a few of the sins you've done…the biggies. Now think about the reality of God's forgiveness that you have received through Jesus Christ.

> By forgiving others we are proving that we accept God's forgiveness and are living within it.

Have you heard about the notion of "Forgive and forget?" It is a myth to some, who truly think it is awful advice. Far better advice to them would be, "Forgive and choose daily whether to walk in forgiveness". You can forgive a person, release them of the guilt of what they have done, and then put up tough boundaries around the relationship in spite of reconciliation. For example, you are not expected to be continually beaten by an abusive man after forgiving him. Let your abuser know that they are forgiven but must seek help from a local pastor or seek other acceptable help. Nowhere in the scripture are we counseled to live the life of a victim. The power of forgiveness is that it enables us to move forward, to live a life that is not strangled by the past. Jesus wants us to have abundant life. Abundant life happens in part when we let go of the past.

> Being unwilling to forgive is like destroying a bridge that we will need to cross ourselves.

It's a risky business to pray, "Forgive us our trespasses as we forgive those who trespass us". Do we really want God to be as forgiving as us? How could we have the nerve to ask for forgiveness if we are unwilling to offer it to others? Being unwilling to forgive is like destroying a bridge that we will need to cross ourselves. A mark of true Christianity—of genuine faith—is the ability to forgive. Haddon Robinson writes, "Those who live in the relief of God's pardon find it easier to forgive those who offend them." Why? Because they have received mercy; they are part of "the forgiveness fellowship". God generously hands out forgiveness to us.

The Apostle John wrote:

> "If we claim to be without sin, we deceive
> Ourselves and the truth is not in us. If we confess
> Our sins, he who is faithful and just will forgive us
> Our sins and cleanse us from all wickedness."—1 John 1 v 8-9

When the Implementation Force (IFOR) traveled through Bosnia, every house they passed had sustained damage from the on-going strife and "ethnic cleansing." Unresolved pain is the result of an unwillingness to forgive. If the people of the Balkans could find peace with God, they could live in peace with one another. Until and unless they can learn forgiveness, the NATO presence is simply delaying another onslaught of violence. Perhaps what is needed is an army of chaplains.

We have an obligation to extend forgiveness to others. People who are unforgiving cannot understand or accept the forgiveness God offers. Anyone who is not willing to forgive another has not experienced God's forgiveness. When we refuse to forgive others, we are asking God not to forgive us. There are many people who refuse to forgive—they harbor resentments and hold grudges. Victims can become bitter, wishing only to get even. People often claim, "I forgive—but I'll never forget!"

> Happy are those who are merciful to others; God will be merciful to them.

When I hear this, I do something unexpected—I urge that person not to forget. I say, "I want you to remember! Every time you remember the offence and feel the hurt, I want you to remember your forgiven sins by the Lord." Amnesia is not the goal! Jesus said in the Beatitudes, "Happy are those who are merciful to others; God will be merciful to them".

With this profound statement in mind by our Lord and the quote from the book of Ezekiel on the onset of this chapter let each and very one of us that harbor resentments, injustice and bitterness over the past generational sins of slavery in America, Western Europe, apartheid in South Africa forgive their own generation because they have nothing to do with it period.

"Because all have sinned and all fall short of the glory of God; and all are graciously forgiven and made righteous through the redemption that is in Christ Jesus."—Apostle Paul (Romans 3 v 23-24)

"I imagine one of the reasons people cling to their hates so stubbornly of others is because they sense, once hate is gone, they will be forced to deal with pain."—James Baldwin

9

When Forgiveness Is Wrong but Right

Many have been jailed most times for offences they knew little or nothing about. Many around the world are jailed for crimes they did not even commit. It is not unusual today in America to learn about people that have been wrongly convicted and incarcerated for twenty plus years only to be released because of the new use of the DNA evidence. Have you been falsely accused and punished for something you knew nothing about? I know it hurts. I've been accused many times in my life for things I knew little or nothing about and I paid sometimes dearly for it. But I

> Don't drag the loads of ill will and resentment one more day.

have learned not to drag the load along. I have offloaded those burdens of hostility and bitterness, and now I'm living free. Learn to live free. It helps you enjoy your days and also enhances your health. Don't drag the loads of ill will and resentment one more day. Forgive from your heart. Free those people from your heart and free yourself in the process. This message by no means undermines these terrible events and atrocities that have accrued in your life. Nonetheless, you must forgive in order for the seed you sow to the Lord to yield abundant blessings.

You might be in jail right now for a crime that you did not commit, or your case is still in court for a false allegation. Genesis chapter 39, verses 6-23, shows us that Joseph was once in similar situation. Joseph's side of the story was not considered because he was a servant but Potiphar's wife's allegation was seen as true because Joseph's garment was found with her.

People were not there while Potiphar's wife was making her advances to Joseph, so he did not have any witnesses. Joseph was subsequently sent to prison. It hurts. Maybe you are like Joseph, currently in jail for an offense you did not commit. The message God wants me to give to you this moment is that you should make up your mind to forgive. God is interested in your case. He asked me to inform you this moment "to make a move'; forgive those people and God will enter. I know it hurts because I've been there myself. Regardless of the circumstances surrounding your own case, you must forgive. Remember it is a question of being right with God, so you may not only receive spiritual healing and financial prosperity but you also receive God himself. I know it is really hard to forgive but it is one of God's major commandments and your key to moving forward in life. In 1st John, chapter 2, verse 4, the Bible says, "if you say, I know Him, but do not fulfill His commands, you are a liar and the truth is not in you." But if you keep his word, God's love is made complete in you. This is how we know that we are in Him."

A recent news story contained a follow up on a shooting that had happened a year earlier. An innocent woman was shot in the cross fire between two men. She became paralyzed by the injury she sustained. The issue concerned the tragic change in her life since the shooting. The thing that struck me most was her statement: "I haven't forgiven them yet, but I know I have to, because if I don't God will not forgive me." I could see the pain that she was in, I could see the life that she had lost, and I wanted to say, "No, God loves you for who you are. You've been severely injured, but it will be all right!" But she knew the truth. Beyond the emotion of seeing a terrible crime such as this, the truth remains that unless we forgive those who have harmed us, who have sinned against us, God will not forgive us.

> Stop being historical. Release anyone who is in the prison of your heart.

She had two things right.

We must forgive to be forgiven. Jesus said that in a number of places, as I take a look at just two of such statements in the New-testament.

In Matthew chapter 7 verse 2 the Lord said;

> "In the same way you judge others,
> you will be judged, and the measure
> you use for others, will be used for you"

In Mark chapter 11 verse 25-26 the Lord said;

> "And when you stand to pray, forgive
> whatever you may hold against anyone,
> so that your heavenly Father may also forgive
> your sins."

The other truth that the woman on the news knew was that forgiveness is difficult. This woman was an athletic, vibrant young woman before the bullet paralyzed her and altered her life forever. How could she forgive that? It is not easy to give up our right to be hurt, to be angry to get back to hate the other for what they have done. You may have had terrible things done to you by someone you love and trusted, and in turn that trust was broken. You may have lost a great deal because of someone's actions. It is not easy to forgive, but by his grace it can be done. We are able to forgive because God is in charge. We are also able to forgive because God takes even the things meant to hurt us, and he uses them for good if we let him; by simply letting it go.

Forgiveness is an act of faith. By forgiving another, you trust that God is a better administer of justice than yourself. By forgiving, you release your right to get even and leave all issues of fairness for God to work out. You leave in God's hands the scales that must balance justice and mercy. Just like tithing is an act of faith by which we are saying, "I might not be able to afford this, but God looks

> By letting go, you trust that God is a better administer of justice than yourself.

after my needs." Forgiveness is an act of faith, because we are saying, "if there is any punishment that is needed, or any giving of mercy, God will look after it just fine."

Jesus lets us know that if we refuse to forgive, then we haven't grasped our great need for forgiveness, or how much God has forgiven us. Thus in our pride, we have not truly repented, and God will not forgive us. But when we have our eyes on the cross, and envision the pain and suffering Jesus went through in order to forgive us and cleanse us from our sins, it can appear pretty minor to forgive those who have harmed us.

We must forgive those who have hurt us because God commands it, our forgiveness hinges on it, and because it is essentially the best thing for us. When we refuse to forgive, the bitterness grows like a cancer within us, eating away at our livelihood causing strain on our emotional and physical well-being. The only therapy for this cancer is the divine surgery of forgiveness. When we refuse to forgive, we allow the sin that was committed against us to hurt us twice; once when we were first sinned against, and again by keeping us from receiving God's forgiveness.

Beloved, is there someone who you need to forgive right now? Is there someone who you haven't talked to in a long time because of what they did? Is there someone who you refused to trust because of what they did? Is there someone who you avoid like the plaque, or someone for whom you just feel like spitting on? Is there someone who you are waiting for a confession from before you offer forgiveness? You must forgive them. Your own forgiveness relies on it.

Karl Menninger, a famed psychiatrist, once said that if he could convince the patients in psychiatric hospitals that their sins were forgiven, seventy-five percent of them could walk out the next day! This is awesome. Most emotional and physical distress can be traced to unforgiveness. Ulcers, high blood pressure migraine headaches, heart attacks, and lower back pain can all arise from the concealment of our sin and the refusal to forgive. Many like dragging these loads of resentment and bitterness. One man was telling his friend about an argument he had with his wife. "Every time we have an argument she gets historical." The friend corrected him and said, "You mean hysterical, don't you? No, I mean historical. Every time we fight she brings up stuff from the past and holds it against me!" God will not get 'historical' with you if you have confessed your sins to him.

The book Psalm chapter 103 verse 12 said:

> "As far as the east is from the west,
> so far has He removed our transgressions from us."

Also in the book of Micah chapter 7 verse 19 the bible echoed:

> "Once again you will show us your loving
> kindness and trample on our wrongs, casting
> our sins into the depths of the sea."

The above verses in the bible indicates clearly that God our heavenly father is not historical with us, so we can not afford to be historical with one another period.

Two friends were walking through the desert. During some point of the journey they had argument, and one friend slapped the other one in the face. The one who got slapped was hurt, but without saying anything, wrote in the sand, "Today my best friend slapped me in the face." They kept on walking until they found an oasis, where they decided to take a bath. The one who had been slapped got stuck in the river and started drowning, but his friend saved him. After he recovered from the near drowning, he wrote on a stone, "Today my best friend saved my life." The friend who had slapped and saved his best friend asked him, "after I hurt you, you wrote in the sand, and now you write on a stone, why?" The other friend replied, "When someone hurts us we should write it down in sand where winds of forgiveness can erase it away. But, when someone does something good for us, we must engrave it in stone where no wind can ever erase it." Learn to forgive the bad and hold on to the good things people do for you. God wants you to forgive and this is required to get your desired healing and prosperity. As He promised us in the book of Joshua, chapter 1 verse 8-9,

> "Constantly read the book of this law and mediate
> on it day and night, that you may do truly what it says
> so that your plans be fulfilled and you shall succeed in
> everything. It is I who commands you; be valiant. Do not
> tremble or be afraid, because Yahweh your God, is with you
> wherever you go."

Some wrongs are easy to forgive. Other wrongs, where we have been used, abused and degraded are not as easy to forgive. Even when we know our Father in heaven wishes it. Deep hurts leave deep scars. Forgiveness isn't easy. Forgiveness is hard, especially in a long term relationship with friends, family or even co-workers that have been plagued with past troubles, tormented by fears of rejection and humiliation, or torn by suspicion and distrust. Even so, it is something that you must do to experience lasting peace and joy in your heart. Real forgiveness doesn't mean that we don't feel hurt. It doesn't mean that we won't do a thing about it every once in a while. It doesn't mean that we won't have a set back on wanting revenge and wanting them to hurt the way we were hurt. It doesn't mean that we have to be their best buddy. It doesn't mean that we will allow them to do it again. It doesn't mean that the pain will go away over night. Our mind has to be filled with the Word of God to such a degree that it writes over the all hurt and any desire for revenge.

One night, a man awoke out of sound sleep, due to a recurring dream. The dream was always the same. He was swimming in a lake, and although a good swimmer, his arms and legs grew increasingly weary, and he feared he might not make it back to shore. Suddenly an elderly man that looked just like his deceased father passed by in a rowboat. He stopped, held out his hand, but recalling how poorly his father treated him as a child, he smiled dryly and said, "No thank you, Dad. I'll be alright."

The man continued to frantically splash his way back to shore. Looking to the side, he saw yet another image in the distance. It was his daughter, swimming quickly toward him with a life preserve. Here, dad! Put them on!" Remembering the many times his daughter disobeyed him as a rebellious teen, the man shook his head and waved his daughter on. Upon finally making it to shore, the man collapsed from exhaustion in the wet sand. Conscious, yet unable to move, the man saw a large group of people around him. All the people looked familiar—faces of the many friends and relations he had come in contact with during his life. They offered to take him to the hospital, to bring him some warm clothes, and other means of assistance, but as each person spoke, the man stood up, brushed off his sandy, wet clothes, and walked wearily into the sunset.

After the third night of dreaming this same dream, the man sought the opinion of the only person he felt he could trust not to hurt him, his wise, old grandmother. "What does the dream mean, gram?" He asked. The elderly and sagacious woman sat in silence for several moments, and then finally spoke. "I'm no dream-reading expert, sonny, but I'd say that someone is trying to tell you that you are holding in a lot of bitterness, due to an unforgiving attitude." The man pounded his fists on the table in indignation. "Bitter? Unforgiving? That is absurd! I should have known better than come to an uneducated woman like you!"

The old woman said very calmly, "There is more. I'm guessing that the struggle you encountered in the water is the same sort of struggle that you often feel inside. You want to reach out and take hold of a warm and caring hand, but no hand is good enough for you. You made it to the shore this time, but what about next time?" Red faced and exasperated, the man stormed out of the room muttering to himself.

Forgiveness is not something we do for others; it is something we do for ourselves. Those who do not forgive others, who do not forgive easily, or who forgive on a conditional basis, slowly build up bitterness internally. Release and relieve yourself today.

When you delete a worthless document on a computer, you make an effort to put it in the computer wastebasket. But it isn't gone from your computer. You must make the additional effort to empty your computer wastebasket. Even then it isn't deleted from your computers memory, it is still there. All your computer did was replaced the first letter with its own code symbol to say it may be overwritten if space becomes needed. It is hidden from you. It can be recovered even then by simply replacing the first letter. Eventually, your computer will write over that file. Only then will it be completely gone. Forgiving others and forgiving yourself is much the same. We have to make a real effort and definite decision to forgive. Then our memory has to be written over. Our mind has to be so filled with the Word of God to the point that it writes over the hurt and desire for revenge. Stop for a moment, go to the recycle bin of the computer of your heart and permanently delete all hurts, resentments and bitterness.

Today, forgiveness is all over the news; Former President Clinton was offered some questionable pardons, and Japan is enraged that the Captain of the naval submarine USS Greenville has not personally apologized for the accident in which the Japanese training ship Ehime Maru was sunk. Are you like the aforementioned Japanese? Are you waiting for personal apology or an open

> Go to the recycle bin of the computer of your heart and permanently delete all hurts, resentments and bitterness.

display of remorse before you forgive? That is not the way to go, release all resentments from your heart immediately. The pay off is much better.

Once upon a time, two brothers who lived on adjoining farms had a serious conflict. They had farmed side by side, shared machinery, and traded labor and goods without a hitch for forty years. A small misunderstanding had widened into a major difference and exploded into an exchange of bitter words.

One morning a carpenter knocked on the older brother's door "I'm looking for a few days of work," he said, "Perhaps you have a few small jobs here and there." "Yes," said the older brother. "Look across the creek at that farm. That's my neighbor; in fact he's my brother. Last week my brother

> Let's learn to go and built bridges instead of walls.

took his bulldozer to the river, Levee, and created this creek between us from what was a meadow. So, I want you to build an 8-foot fence so I won't need to see his place any-more." The carpenter said, "I think I understand the situation."

The older brother helped the carpenter get the materials ready and then he disappeared. The carpenter worked hard all day measuring, sawing, and nailing. It was about sunset when the farmer returned, his eyes open wide, and his jaw dropped. A bridge—with handrails and all—stretched from one side of the creek to another. His younger brother was now also gazing at the bridge in amazement. The younger brother then said; "You are quite a brother to build this bridge after all I've said and done." The two broth-ers stood at each end of the bridge, met in the middle, and then shook each other's hand. They turned to see the carpenter leave. "No, wait, stay a few days, I've a lot of projects for you to do," said the older brother. The carpenter replied, "I'd love to stay, but I have many bridges to build." Let's learn to let go and build bridges instead of walls.

The Pastor of an evangelical church near Orlando, Florida had been lead-ing the same flock for more than twelve years. Things were running smoothly except for the fact that one member, an influential banker, was constantly questioning his authority on business matters. When the banker was nominated to become a deacon, the pastor stood before the congregation and said. "I don't believe this man is qualified to be elected." Then he read a long list of instances where the man had questioned his decision. The congregation didn't agree with him and voted the banker in. Soon everyone in the church thought lower of him. Within six months, the pastor resigned.

Don't be like this pastor. If you are occupying a position of leadership, don't let anger take control of you and your decisions. Did you know that being angry (refusing forgiveness) is a sin? It is all right to be angry. God gave you that emotion but when something wrong or unfair happens to you, don't sin by not forgiving and don't let your anger take control of you. Refusing forgiveness and harboring ill feeling towards someone can eat at you like the cancer described earlier.

Let's look into God's own holy Word. I would like to direct your attention to the book of Luke chapter 15 verses 11-24, the parable of the prodigal son. He had caused his father some pain but when he came to his senses in verse 18, he decided to go home to his father and say, "Father, I have sinned against heaven and against you, And I am no longer worthy to be called your son. Make me like one of your hired servants." But look at what happens in verse 21. Even before the boy can get those apologetic words out of his mouth...the father runs up to him and embraces him. Folks, that is a strong indication that the dad had already forgiven his wayward son before he could even say, "I'm sorry." God is the father in that story, and we sinners are the wayward son. Okay...but that son in the parable was sorry for the hurt and pain he had caused. What about the people who are not sorry or repentant? Remember that in verse 21, the father did not wait for the son to analyze and apologize; he had already forgiven even before he came. You can do likewise this very moment. Forgive and offload any form of hurt, resentment and bitterness even if the person involved did not show remorse or come to you to apologize. When Jesus was dying on the cross, he looked down at the people who had mocked, rejected and crucified Him yet He prayed for their forgiveness. (Luke 23:34). For all we know, many of these people went to their graves without ever acknowledging their sins and without ever asking for forgiveness, and yet Jesus prayed for their forgiveness.

> "But I say to you who hear me:
> Love your enemies and do good to those
> who hate you. Bless those who curse you and
> pray for those who treat you badly." (Luke 6 v 27-28)

Who is it that Jesus says we're supposed to do all these nice things to? Repentant friends or apologetic family members? No...your enemies! Can we safely assume that an enemy is someone who is not sorry for hurting us…and is not about to ask for forgiveness? You better believe it! Yet Jesus says to treat them in ways that sure sound to me like total forgiveness. It doesn't matter if that person remains an enemy and refuses to seek forgiveness. This has nothing to do with the miracle of forgiveness in your own heart. Our only job is to forgive, and leave that other person's attitude in God's hands.

Barbarians, cavemen and headhunters do not forgive. It takes a wise, kind, and godly person to forgive. Let's take a look at the story of Joseph in Genesis, chapter 37. Joseph's brothers hated him, and one day made up their mind to get rid of him. Their plot to kill him foiled, but they sold him out to the Ishmaelite for twenty pieces of silver. That was how Joseph got to Egypt. In Egypt, he was in Potiphar's house. In Genesis, chapter 39, we see Joseph being sent to prison for an offense he did not commit. It was in this prison where he met with the chief butler and interpreted his dream. The bible said that the chief butler did forget him after two years of leaving prison. In Genesis, chapter 41, the chief butler remembered Joseph when the king had a dream that nobody could interpret. The interpretation of the King's dream brought Joseph the promotion of a lifetime. He was elevated to the highest position in the land. In Genesis 42, we see his brothers came down to Egypt to buy grains when the famine was biting hard. When they arrived, Joseph recognized them but they did not.

Who could blame Joseph if he had reacted negatively, answered rudely, and behaved cruelly? If physical, emotional, and mental abuse were not options, he could have at least scolded, criticized, or warned them to shape up or ship out, and not to count their chickens or blessings so fast. Joseph cried from his heart for his brothers. Most of us might cry for the wayward brothers, but not with them; we might speak to them, but not with them; and may shake their hands, but not embrace them. Some of us would make them writes lines, do community service, or take hatred, jealousy, and lying management classes. However, a forgiving person offers a bandage to people in bondage—the kind of bandage that heals wounds, scars and incisions.

After Joseph made himself known to his brothers, the past still haunted them. Joseph's brothers finally confessed to a family secret they have harbored for more than twenty years. They were perennial hostage to their hatred, jealousy and lies. Joseph not only forgave his brothers in words, he treated them kindly. He loved them, hugged them, and kissed them. He knew they were stricken in their hearts, scared out of their mind, and shaking their heads in disbelief. He counseled them not to be distressed and angry with themselves and not to blame, criticize, or fight one another (Gen 45:24)

Forgiveness is not cheap grace, empty talk, or trouble-free. Many years had passed since the brothers arrived in Egypt. Their fathers passed away in Egypt after seventeen years in the new country. (Genesis 47: 28). After the funeral, the brothers again begged for Joseph's forgiveness. They were afraid that reality, regret, and repercussions might set in, and Joseph would show resentment, demand reparation, and pursue revenge. The brothers did not understand that the path to forgiveness was completed seventeen years ago (Gen 41:46, 53) when they returned with Benjamin. The death of their father did nothing to cancel or annul Joseph's forgiveness. Joseph never regretted forgiving his brothers. When he forgave them seventeen years ago, he forgave them consciously, compassionately, and continuously. He meant his word, decision and stance—not for his father's sake, but for their sake, and not out of his sympathy for them, but out of God's kindness to him. Joseph made a decision to commute his brothers' sentence,

> Forgiveness is not based on merit, but out of grace and love.

shorten their sorrow, and expunge their record there and then. Amazingly, Joseph never mentioned to Jacob his betrayal, slavery, or imprisonment. The past that haunted the brothers for the twenty-two years of Joseph's disappearance was more than adequate punishment by itself.

Forgiveness is not based on merit, but out of grace and love. The barriers were removed and the bridge was built when Joseph reunited with his brothers. There was no reason to rehearse, revisit, or reverse the past now. Forgiveness brings healing. It sets someone free from the chains, burdens and years of bondage. Have you hated, despised, and begrudged someone for weeks, months, and years? Set them free, find relief for yourself, and make brothers of your enemies.

A long time ago, a newly married girl named Li-li could not get along with her mother-in-law who now lived with the newlyweds. Their personalities and habits clashed tremendously. They never stop arguing and fighting. Traditionally, Li-li had to bow to her mother-in-law and obey her every wish. Finally, Li-li could not stand her mother-in-law's temperament and dictatorship any longer.

Li-li went to see a family friend, Mr. Huang, who also sold herbs. After telling him the situation, she asked for some poison to slip into her mother-in-law's meals. She even agreed to do whatever Mr. Huang told her. Mr. Huang then gave her a package of herbs and told Li-li, "To eliminate suspicion, I have given you a number of herbs to slowly build up poison in her body. Every other day prepare some pork or chicken and put a little of these herbs in her food. Also, act very friendly towards her so that nobody suspects you when she dies. Don't argue with her, obey her every wish, and treat her like a queen."

Li-li began serving the specially prepared food to her mother-in-law. She controlled her temper, obeyed her mother-in-law, and treated her like her own mother. For the next six months, Li-li was rarely upset and the arguments with her friendlier and more jovial mother-in-law were few and far between an argument with her kindler and friendlier mother-in-law. They were like mother and daughter. In horror, Li-li came to Mr. Huang and pleaded tearfully, "Mr. Huang, please help me to keep the poison from killing my own mother-in-law. She's change into such a nice woman, and I love her like my own mother. I don't want her to die." Mr. Huang comforted her, "Li-li, I never gave you any poison. I gave you vitamins to improve her health. The only poison had been in your mind and your attitude."

Are you still throwing eggs, bricks, or daggers at others? Have you applied bandages on yourself or on those who hurt you? Are you still building walls?

How does the suffering and salvation of Jesus Christ affect your relationship with the unloving, the unkind, the people whose personalities and habits clash with yours, and the ungracious? We have seen forgiveness illustrated and analyzed in different life experiences and Biblical instances. One question which might arise, "How can I forgive someone who is dead or that I have lost track of? You have to know one thing; forgiving someone is not contingent on whether they seek to receive that forgiveness. It's something we're supposed to do in our hearts regardless of the other person's attitude.

I know what you're thinking. "God is perfect and Holy, I'm a sinner. I can never forgive the way God does." You're right. On your own, you can never follow God's example of unwavering and absolute forgiveness. As noted earlier one of the verses in Psalm 51 reads "Create in me a clean heart, O God, and renew a right spirit within me." The Holy Spirit can create that kind of forgiving heart within us; if we will just let him! Beloved, you are not reading this by mistake. God wants you to have supernatural healing and prosperity. The access required to accept these blessings can be granted if you open your heart at this moment and preventively remove all negativity, hate, and resentment. Again, God is more than willing to release your supernatural healing and prosperity, but you must make your life a fertile soil.

"For you Lord are good and ready to forgive and abundant in mercy to all those who call upon you."…King David (Psalm 86 v 5)

"You may be sorry that you spoke, sorry that you stayed or left, sorry you won or lost, sorry so much was spent. But as you go through life, you will find that you were never sorry that you were kind and forgiving."—Herbert Prochnow

10

Forgiving the Unexpected

Dealing with the disappointment and despair of those you trust the most is especially tasking. People such as your best friend or someone whom you believe that you are in love with. These two inspirational stories will guide and show you how to deal with these situations.

Absolute forgiveness is a cure to those who envy you for your blessings and success. This is best illustrated by this first story of Marie, a writer from Sherman Oaks, California.

The story began when one day Marie called her very good friend to wish her a happy birthday. Her friend's response was a sudden attack on her. Her friend ridiculed her, and gave her a long list of the things she did which bothered her. This phone conversation ultimately severed their long-time relationship.

> Absolute forgiveness is a cure to those who envy you for your blessings and success.

Marie was completely taken aback by her friend's reaction. Her career was going extremely well, with a book soon to be released and a number of accolades for her essays. She believes that her friend did not like all these success and became envious.

Meanwhile, Marie spent two years being upset. Anytime she ran into her ex-best friend, her heart would pound and she would get so tensed up that she felt sick. Who among us has felt betrayed, unfairly treated, or wronged for no reason? For many of us, our natural initial reaction is to cling to the rage, bitterness and pain.

Marie's healing began when she happened to meet her estranged friend. She confronted her friend and politely told her how badly she had hurt her. Her estranged friend listened but did not offer any apology. Marie even surprised herself by asking her friend to forgive her for all the hate, anger and bitterness she had towards her during this period. It was during this unpleasant time, when she realized the ultimate peace one gets when one forgives, and absent of any reciprocal apology from her friend.

Her experience is in line with the findings of Fred Luskin, PhD, director of Stanford Forgiveness Project and author of Forgiveness for Good. Luskin pointed out that forgiveness does not mean that one is condoning the offense. But found that when one lets go of bitterness and grudge, one can slash their stress level by up to fifty percent. Those that vol-

> Hauling a load of hate and resentments can become disturbingly unhealthy.

unteer in this study have also shown an increase in energy, overall sleep quality, and an overall physical vitality. Hauling a load of hate and resentments can become disturbingly unhealthy. Science is now coming in line with what the bible has emphasized over and over again.

The second story is about Millie and Yemi, best friends who were also cousins. They were very close, and it was a very spiritual relationship. They had this incredible, inseparable bond, constantly discussing issues that no one in their families and friends were interested in.

Millie and Yemi were more than best friends and yet different than family. They had their own language that the family could not understand even if they tried.

At the age of 18, Millie and her boyfriend Jimmy planned to get married. Yemi and Jimmy hated each other for years, despite Millie's tireless efforts to unite them.

Jimmy was a very generous person. He was always buying expensive trinkets and jewelry for Millie. She had no interest at all in them. She simply said "thank you" and put them in her jewelry box. Yemi thought that Millie was crazy because she has a "goldmine" mentality.

One day Millie discovered that Jimmy was having an affair with another girl from their crowd. All her friends knew about it except for Yemi who then have moved to another state. The first person Millie consults about the affair is Yemi who advises Millie to join her in the state where she resides.

Millie spent the entire summer venting to Yemi of how "torn" she was, but was still willing to forgive Jimmy because she loved him so much. Meanwhile, Jimmy constantly called and begged Millie for forgiveness. Yemi on the other hand, was trying her best to make sure their reconciliation did not occur. The main reason being, that she was trying to start her own relationship with Jimmy behind Millie's back.

While Jimmy was busy asking Yemi to put in a good word for him, she was busy trying to court him. She told him that his past relationship was a lost cause since Millie has already moved on. Jimmy and Yemi eventually began a relationship. When Millie found out she walked away from both of them crushed and bitter as one could expect.

Millie did not talk to both of them over the years. As with most instances like this, the relationship between Jimmy and Yemi ended. After some years had passed, Millie would sometimes run into Jimmy and exchange pleasantries, but refused to speak to Yemi. As long time friends, Millie expected more from Yemi and simply could not find it in her heart to forgive her, even many years after the event. Jimmy, now in his late thirties, was starting to have a failing health and needed a heart transplant. Millie and her husband kept in close touch with him for moral support. Jimmy always pleaded with Millie to call Yemi her cousin and let bygones be bygones. Millie would just tell him to mind his business.

Not too long after Jimmy was released from the hospital after his heart transplant, he called Millie to inform her that Yemi, now thirty-four years old, was dying of cancer and only had two months to live. Millie hung up the phone in shock and disbelief. She knew then, she must forgive and go see her best friend and cousin Yemi.

When Millie and Yemi finally got together, they both wept profusely as they could not believe that it took a terminal illness such as cancer to bring them back together.

Over the next few months Millie became a caretaker for Yemi. Cleaning her up when she became sick. One day, Yemi told her that she has been wondering about Jesus lately. Millie was surprise because they were both Jewish. So Millie picked up a bible and started reading the New Testament to her best friend.

Yemi eventually passed on, but only after both had forgiven the other and renewed their love and friendship. Over the next several months, after her best friend passed on, Millie became depressed thinking about the number of years she missed out because of her unforgiving attitude.

Let these stories inspire you. Do not wait for a tragic event like cancer to occur before you forgive, especially those you love and trust.

"Whoever conceals his faults will not prosper, but he who confesses and renounces them will be shown mercy."...King Solomon (Proverbs 28 v 13)

"To forgive is the highest, most beautiful form of love. In return, you will receive untold peace and happiness."—Robert Muller

11

Freedom of Forgiveness

"I had a brother once, and I betrayed him." With these words, African writer Laurens Van Der Post begins the wonderful book, "The Seed and the Sower"; The story is about two brothers from a small South African village. The elder brother is tall, athletic, intelligent and a natural leader. The younger brother lacked these characteristics. He had a back deformity, which he was very sensitive of, but he possessed a beautiful singing voice. They both attended the same private school. One night, some of the older boys drugged the younger brother outside, ripped off his shirt, and made fun of his deformity until he cried. They threw him into an abandoned water tank and forced him to sing. The older brother was aware of what was going on but did nothing to rescue his younger brother. The younger brother survived but his spirit was crushed. He returned to the family farm and lived a solitary life, refusing to ever sing again. During World War II, the older brother had a dream in which he realized he had been Judas to his younger brother. He makes the incredibly difficult journey back to South Africa and asks his brother's forgiveness. Later that night, in the dark of the night, he hears a beautiful sound—it is his brother singing a song that the older brother had written when they were boys.

In this story, the younger brother had a choice to make when his older brother asked his forgiveness. He could forgive him or he could hold on to the hurt, bitterness, resentment and anger and refuse his forgiveness. But let me ask you a question—who is held captive then? In the prison of resentment, bitterness, anger and revenge, who is really imprisoned? If he holds on to bitterness, whose soul is paralyzed? Whose mind is held in bondage? Whose emotions are frozen? If the younger brother decides to hold on to the pain, to the resentment and the desire for revenge, all he will gain is self-centered pain. In films, bounty hunters are always seen riding alone, which poses the question, "Who wants to be friends with someone who settles scores for a living?"

Holding on to the bitterness of the past is like knowing how to ride a bicycle without knowing how to stop. You just continue to pedal, on and on, afraid and unable to stop, but desperately hoping that someone pulls the brakes and saves you from the sure-fire collision. And what if you get revenge, then what? Is justice satisfied? Are you released from all the pain? Does the resentment disappear? Does the open wound suddenly close up and heal itself? The answer of course is no, therefore let it go.

In the book of Colossians, around 60 AD, Paul wrote to the church to refute some false teaching. He never explicitly mentioned the false teaching, but from the letter we can deduce that it contained ceremonialism, asceticism, angel worship, secret knowledge and a reliance on human wisdom and traditions over and against the gospel of Christ.

Paul wrote to the believers at Colossians asking them to clothe themselves with virtues. They would need to bear with those whose faults which irritated them. They would need to forgive those who sinned against them. They should put the garment of love upon one another, which reflects their love for Christ.

> The issue is not the existence of the pain, injury or injustice, but rather the treatment of it.

Jesus spoke from the cross on Calvary's hill—"Father forgive them." There was no questioning the reality of his wounds. There was no doubting the pain of the injury or the injustice. There was no doubt that he was sinned against, that he was innocent. The same is true for us. Jesus does not doubt your pain. He does not deny the reality of the injury or the injustice. He does not refute the fact that you are innocent. The issue is not the *existence* of the pain, injury or injustice, but rather the *treatment* of the pain, injury, or injustice.

Let's examine some practical questions. What are you going to do with your debts? I don't mean your financial debts. What are you going to do with the debt of pain, injury, hurt and injustice that people have committed against you? How you answer this question may affect your walk with God. It can also determine your witness of God before man and your contentment in life.

So what are we to do? Let me suggest to you that the Scripture is clear—we are to forgive those who have sinned against us as we have been forgiven by God our Father. Colossians 3, verse 13, is in fact an echo of the Lord's Prayer and an echo of Christ's words from the Cross. Let me say to you again—God does not deny your pain. He does not deny the hurt, the injury or the injustice. However, He said; as indicated to earlier on, that vengeance is his and his alone. Revenge is such a lonely and unhealthy occupation. When you put someone in your jail of resentment and hatred, you only imprison yourself. The prisoner has the freedom to walk around, while you on the other hand, become emotionally traumatized.

God is omniscient, He knows all things and he remembers all things. As also, indicated in somewhere else in this book. In Psalm 103 God said to us "I will not hold your past against you." God does forgive and forget. He forgives and he makes the choice to remember no more—not to hold it against us. Forgiving is not forgetting. Forgetting may be a long term by-product of forgiving, but it is not the same. God says to each of us, "I will not let the past dictate the present." It does not mean He will tolerate sin or that we should. He takes, and we should take, a stand against future sin whilst forgiving past sin.

You can choose to live in the Bondage of Bitterness or the Freedom of Forgiveness. You can choose to forgive in order to bring healing into your life and into theirs. You do not heal in order to forgive; you forgive in order to heal. Through forgiveness, you are consciously refusing to allow the past to dictate how you live in the present or the future. It is as much for your sake as it is for their sake. You are as much the captive as they are. We are no longer a product of our pasts—we are new creations in Christ. Evaluate your past in light of the redemptive work of Jesus Christ. It is who you are now in Christ as opposed to who you were then.

I am not trivializing the pain, the injury or the injustice. Forgiveness is a process. It is a series of steps, some of which require frequent retracing. It does take time. It is the restoring of an attitude of love and a releasing of a painful past. It repudiates revenge and reopens the future to the possibility of a restored relationship. It is costly and hard. It is not tolerance. It is not 'make-believe', as if it didn't happen or matter. There is a difference between forgiveness and a tired memory. Paul says in Corinthians 2, verses 10-11, "Nothing keeps us in bondage to the past as much as our unwillingness to forgive." The refusal to forgive leads to bitterness of the soul, which in turn leads to spiritual death.

> Evaluate your past in light of the redemptive work of Jesus Christ.

DEVELOPING THE ART OF FORGIVENESS

I want to give you some practical points for developing the art of forgiveness in your own life. As Christians, we do not need to look far to develop this art. All we have to do is study the word of our Lord Jesus Christ and always ask ourselves what our Lord will do in any given situation.

Think of Christ's suffering. Think of what he endured. Now ask yourself—"How does the way I have been wronged compare to the way Christ was wronged." This may help to gain some perspective.

Recall the many kind deeds shown to you, perhaps even by the person who has harmed you.

Make a list of the good things you have received from the Lord.

Thank him for blessing you with his love and forgiveness each day.

Make an honest effort to pray for the one who has hurt or injured you.

Go even further by looking for an opportunity to help them.

If the offence is especially hard to forget, pray for God's grace to replace the memory by giving you gracious and generous thoughts.

Before you fall asleep at night, slowly and thoughtfully repeat the phrase from the Lord's Prayer, "Forgive us our debts, as we forgive our debtors.

THE PROCESS OF FORGIVENESS

Make a conscious decision not to seek revenge or nurse a grudge, and decide instead to forgive (Conversion of the heart).

Think differently about the offender and do your best to talk things over with them.

Accept the pain you have experience without passing it onto other, including the offender.

Think about how it feels to be released from a burden or grudge.

Seek meaning in the suffering you have experienced.

Vision the offender as a tool that God is using to build up your character.

Realize the paradox of forgiveness: as you LET IT GO and forgive the offender, you will experience release and healing.

KEYS TO WALKING IN FORGIVENESS

The keys to walking in forgiveness is to equip yourself with different verses in the word of God, both in the new and old testaments. The verses listed below are just a few. Familiarize yourself with these verses and gather more as you study the word.

Proverbs chapter 19 verse 11:

> "A clever man is slow to anger,
> his glory lies in forgetting offenses"

Proverbs chapter 24 verse 29:

> "Do not say, I will do to him what
> he did to me; I will repay him for his deeds."

Colossians chapter 3 verse 12-13:

> "Therefore as the elect of God, holy and beloved,
> put on tender mercies, kindness, humility, meekness,
> longsuffering, bearing with one another, and forgiving
> One another when there is occasion to do so. As the Lord
> has forgiven you, forgive one another."

There is no limit to forgiveness as indicated in the book of:

Matthew chapter 18 verse 21:

> "Then Peter came to Him and said, "Lord, how
> often shall my brother sin against me, and I forgive
> him? Jesus said to him, "I do not say to you, up to
> Seven times, but up to seventy times seven."

Jesus didn't mean forgive 490 times and stop; it is limitless. How many times do you want to be forgiven?

Proverbs 28 verse 13:

> "He who covers his sins will not prosper, but
> Whosoever confess and forsakes them will have mercy."

Unforgiveness is a sin, which blocks prosperity.

Forgiveness is not a feeling but a decision. It is continual (past, present, and future). It is of the spirit—not the flesh, and not the soul. You must be able to see your offender as a living spirit, not an enemy, not some challenge on life's little mercy way, and not just a speed bump on your road to paradise.

> Reconciliation is always the answer.

Reconciliation is always the answer.

We cannot afford any areas of unforgiveness in our life. We must keep our conscience clear and keep ourselves reconciled to others. Don't dwell on it. Command your soul to be a subject to your spirit.

There was once a Pastor who arrived at his new church and on his first Sunday in the pulpit, he delivered a powerful sermon that truly endeared the congregation to him. On the way out of church, many of the people thanked the Pastor for that Sermon. The next Sunday, he preached another powerful sermon. A few people noticed that it was the exact same sermon from the week before. It seemed a little strange, but nobody mentioned it. They just filed out and thanked the Pastor for another job well done. Well, this went on for several weeks. Finally, one of the Elders got up during the service and said to the Pastor, "You know, you've preached the same sermon for the past month, how many more times are you planning to preach it? The minister responded, "I'll quit preaching it, when you folks start living it!" That sermon was on forgiveness.

"Peace be with you; I give you my peace. Not as the world gives peace do I give it to you. Do not be troubled; do not be afraid."...Lord Jesus Christ (John 14 v 27)

"Anger will never disappear so long as thoughts of resentment are cherished in the mind. Anger will disappear just as soon as thoughts of resentment are forgotten."—Isabelle Holland

12

Forgiveness and Restoration

When you forgive, you must do it wholeheartedly. In the event of an auto accident, the goal of the insurance policy is to bring you back to whole, bring you back to your former good position.

For example, let's assume you were involved in a major car accident where your car was severely damaged and you suffered some physical injury. The insurance company will write off your car, compensate you with the value of the car prior to the wreck, and pay the medical bills for any injury you incurred, all with the objective of bringing you back to whole. Similarly, when you forgive, you must bring to whole and start anew where you left before the enemy tried to break you off. If you were close friends before the rift, then after you have forgiven the person you need start doing the activities you participated in before, such as going to movies, playing card games. If you are married and both of you are still

> Children are adversely affected, even into their adulthood, when they experienced a bitter family break-up.

in love with each other, then you should seek counseling and get back together. If however one person has moved on, and children are involved, do plan at least once or twice a month to do something together as a family. When you do this, you are healing yourself and your children. Children are adversely affected, even into their adulthood, when they experienced a bitter family break-up. That is exactly what the enemy likes to see. Do not give the devil that opportunity. The bible said, "Resist the devil and he will flee from you." Be childlike in your forgiveness.

I watch my little daughters play and fight all the time. Through my vigilant eyes, I have developed some spiritual understanding to what Jesus meant in the book of Matthew chapter 18 verse 3, when He said:

> "I assure you unless you change and
> become like little children, you cannot enter
> Into the kingdom heaven."

They always offend each other and make each other upset. But no matter how many offenses occur per day, once they tell each other they are sorry, that is the end of it. Those of you that have young children, observe them when they play and fight and you will understand what I mean.

Children always forgive and forget and go on with the task at hand. Their forgiveness for one another is final. They do not bring past offenses up as we do as adults. It is done; they go on with their business. That is what God expects of us who are much more mature.

I give you another quick story. One evening, I went to pick up my two young girls, Tunika and Temishi, from school. I noticed that Tunika had this rather large cut on her cheek. It appeared as if someone had sliced her with a blade, leaving this long, deep cut on her cheek. My first reaction was unbelief and anger. The teacher went on and told me how a fellow five-year-old used his razor-sharp fingernail to cut her while they were playing. The problem with this cut was that it took a long time to heal. But each time I went to pick up my girls from school, they were always playing with the same boy. One day I told Tunika, "You must be careful with this boy before you get cut again." She candidly replied, "But daddy, he already said he was sorry." That truly moved me, and then God spoke to me, "That is the kind of forgiveness I am talking about."

> Children always forgive and forget and go on with the task at hand. Their forgiveness for one another is final.

There I was, worrying about the scar developing on her cheek, but she had already forgiven the boy and the two continued about their business. That is the kind of forgiveness our Lord refers to. If you do not forgive, and bring things back to normal, to whosoever you claim you have forgiven, God sees that you are dishonest. So do not deceive yourself and attest that you have forgiven someone when you still hold grudges or malice.

After you have forgiven, completely let go and restore the broken relationship. Only then will you be ready to sow into God's kingdom. We know you will fall many times, just as toddlers learning to walk. You must persevere and continue to ask our Lord for his forgiveness and Fatherly love. Then, get ready to obtain your promised treasure as voiced by God in the book of Isaiah chapter 45 verse 3:

> "I will give you treasures hidden in darkness
> and riches stored in secret places, so the you
> may know that I am Yahweh the God of Israel who
> Calls you by your name."

"There for if you bring your gift to the altar and remember that your brother has something against you, leave your gift there before the altar and go your way. First be reconciled to your brother and then come and offer your gift."...Lord Jesus Christ (Matthew 5 v 23-24)

"We attached our feeling to the moment when we were Hurt, Endowing it with immortality. And we let it assault us every time it comes to mind. It travels with us, sleeps with us, hovers over us while we make love, and broods over us while we die. Our hate does not even have the decency to die when those we hate dies—for it is a parasite sucking our blood, not theirs. There is only one remedy for it-forgiveness."—Lewis B. Smedes

13

You Can Sow

After you have genuinely forgiven from your heart, then you can sow your seed. **"A seed will meet a need"**. The Bible indicated in the book of Genesis chapter 8 verse 22;

> "As long as the earth lasts,
> seed time and harvest, cold and heat,
> summer and winter, day and night
> shall not cease."

Maybe your seed did not been bring your expected harvest because of your unforgiving heart. Now that you have taken care of it, your harvest is guaranteed.

But you may ask yourself, "How much do I sow? Then Bible voiced in Ecclesiastes chapter 11 verses 4-6 when it said:

> "He who watches the wind will not sow,
> and he who watches the cloud will not reap.
> As you do not know what the way of the wind
> Or how the bones grow in the womb of her who
> is with a child, so you do not know anything about
> the works of God who makes everything.
> In the morning sow your seed and do not be idle in
> the evening for you do not know whether one or the
> other will succeed. What if both prove to be good?"

93

2nd Corinthians chapter 9 verses 6-7 indicated that:

> "He who sows sparingly shall also reap
> sparingly and he who sow bountifully shall reap
> bountifully. So let each give as he purposes in his
> Heart not grindingly or of necessity; for God loves a
> cheerful givers."

When we are give or sow, we should give with a cheerful heart, not grudgingly, because God is after the heart.

The Bible also said in Malachi chapter 3, verse 10;

> "Bring you all the tithes in the store house, that there
> may be meat in my house, and prove me here, says the Lord
> Of hosts, if I will not open for you the windows of heaven and
> pour out for you such blessings that there will no be room
> enough to receive it."

Before I got called into the ministry, I really had a problem with this principle. In of this scripture, God is asking us to plant at least ten percent of our seed in churches or ministries and watch him open the doors and windows (opportunities) of heaven in order to bless us. I decided to try it out for only a certain period of time, but have continued till this day. The result has been amazing. My business took off in that year, and I made more money than ever before. Believe you me, it works, everything about the word of God works.

> When we give or sow, we should give with a cheerful heart, not grudgingly, because God is after the heart.

The most important gift I have received from the Lord is being called into his ministry. My first call, I now believe was around mid December 1993 after I had sold a piece of land to a church. The church building has since been built on the said land. The very night after I completed the transaction, I had a dream in which Jesus came into the very room I was sleeping.

He wore a brilliant white garment and held an object resembling a broom, without uttering a word, he slowly paced around my bed, I was completely petrified, yet joyful. When I woke up, I ran to my best friend's room to tell him about my wonderful dream, only to have him question my sanity. Despite his skepticism, I remained spellbound. It was absolutely incredible. Words are still inadequate to explain this dream. It is better experienced than described, and could certainly happen to you too.

His second appearance to my family and I, was what we believe strongly to be an image of Jesus Christ captured on amateur video. The video was taken August 3rd, 2002, at a mobile home park, in a small town called Thelma, California, located near Palm Springs. You can get a copy of this video from our ministry for a donation of any amount. Once you view this video, your life may be forever changed. Better still, you can also visit Thelma in Southern California where this supernatural, massive cross is appearing even as you read. When you go, you are encouraged to go with various types of cameras, video recorders, and the like because the Lord might just have a surprise for you.

Thousands of people have already visited the site. There has been healing, answered prayers, miracles upon miracles, and the Lord revealing himself in different formats and to different visitors. You are encouraged to go and see how he might reveal Himself to you. Pray and prepare yourself before you go.

All these appearances did not convince me of his call until I met a man of God in Nigeria during a visit in November of 2002. He told me that I am running away from a ministry that God had called me into. He said, I needed to stop running and heed to God's calling. Maybe as you are reading this, God is calling you to spread his word. Your answer should be YES. As part of his spiritual blessing for you, refrain from running away as I did, and instead, become a partner with this ministry or form your own ministry and help spread the gospel of Jesus Christ.

When I was planting seeds for my lawn as described in the preface, I planted the seeds all over. The concept or idea here is rather simple; you should sow well. I did not plant on half of the ground, hoping that the other half will miraculously grow. God wants all of us to help spread his message and win souls for him. Do you know that more than half of the world population does not know our Lord and Savior Christ? We are talking about three billion out of six billion plus people in the world today. When you sow into this ministry and help us win souls for Jesus and follow the principle of forgiveness, love and patience, God will give you the spiritual and any other blessings you are seeking, make no mistake about that.

When you sow, I would like you to write or email us as to what you are seeking from the Lord, so that we may pray with you. You should always sow, do not only sow when you need something. Once you get your salary or wage, set aside God's money immediately and send it to your church or any biblical base charity organization of your choice. When you do this, you are consistently following God's instructions, and you will continue to receive his blessing. Blessing comes in different formats. You might pray for your family to get back together, if it is the best thing for you, God will make it happen. You might be sowing for healing; God will also make it happen because with God all things are possible. Whatever your aspirations are, a truly forgiving heart will allow you to begin sowing your seed and receive God's continuous blessings.

"Love is patient, kind, without envy, it is not boastful or arrogant. It is not ill-mannered nor does it seek its own interest. Love overcomes anger and forgets offences. It does not take delight in wrong, but rejoices in truth. Love excuses everything, believes all things, hopes in all things and endures all things. Love will never end."...Apostle Paul (1 Corinthians 13 v 4-8)

"Children should be taught love and forgiveness very early in life and this should be done in the family setting. A family should be a place where love and forgiveness are experienced and understood, so that they will in turn do the same in their life time."

14

The Power of Love

Apart from good soil, water is also needed for our seed to grow. Similarly, after forgiveness, LOVE is the next beautiful thing required for the sown seed in the spiritual rim to grow. In the book of Mark chapter 12 verses 29-31, in response to the question of which commandment is the greatest? Jesus answered:

> "The first of all commandments is: Hear, O
> Israel, the Lord our God, the Lord is one. And
> you shall love the Lord your God with all your
> heart, with all your soul, with your entire mind and
> with all your strength. This is the first commandment.
> And the second, like it, is this; you shall love your neighbors
> as yourself. There is no other commandment greater than these."

If we really love each other as we love ourselves, most of our problems would become a thing of the past. But the enemy will always come with his lies, deceptions and jealousy, and use these to impede our God-promised blessings. The greatest act of love is shown to us in the bible, as indicated in the famous book of John chapter 3 verse 16:

> Love is patient, kind, without envy, it is not boastful or arrogant.

> "For God so loved the world that He gave
> His only begotten Son that whosoever believe
> in Him shall not perish but have an everlasting life."

If you have truly forgiven those that have hurt you, you must then show them love. You should give them love, and your love for them must be sincere. You cannot say you have forgiven but continue to have hatred in your heart. I know it is difficult to forgive, and at the same time love those that have caused you so much emotional or even physical pain. But remember the emotional and physical pain that Jesus went through when he died for our sins at the cross as indicated throughout this book. Before he died that painful death at Calvary, he said, "Father forgive them for they know not what they were doing." We have to do the same to those that have sinned against us; forgive and love them for they don't know what they are doing either.

> You are the light of the world; show this by showing love to one another.

In Matthew chapter 5 verse 45-46 (Amplified version) Jesus said;

> "If you love those who love you, what is?
> Special about that? Do not even tax collectors
> so as much? If you are friendly only to your friends,
> What is so exceptional about that? Do not even pagans
> do as much? For your part you shall be righteous and perfect
> in the way your heavenly father is righteous."

What the Lord Jesus is teaching us here is that we should not only show love to the people that we have forgiven, or our family members and relatives, but also to strangers that we meet on a daily basis. You might see someone in the grocery store that needs help, render your help. If you have someone new at the job, give them a helping hand. Even if it the person was promoted over you and you felt they were unqualified; continue to show them love. If you see some one whose car have broken down render your help. Any opportunity that presents itself for you to help out, do it. Do not hesitate to render love and kindness at all times.

In 1st Peter chapter 4, verse 8-9 said;

"Above all, let your love for one another be sincere,
for love covers a multitude of sins. Welcome one another
Into your houses without complaining."

Some years back, my first job after I graduated from college was being a manager in a retail store. I was doing my rounds in the store one afternoon when a young pregnant woman approached me. She was then in her early twenties. I thought she was about to have the baby because of the pain expressed on her face. I said to her, "can I help you?" She said yes but not as you think". She went on to tell me that she, her husband, and her then three-year old son were sleeping in the car. Her husband had lost his job and they had ran out of money paying for different motels. It has becoming unbearable for her to sleep in the car. "Can you please help us?" she asked. Overwhelmed with compassion, I moved them into my apartment and allowed them to stay with me for a few months. She had her baby and once her husband got a new job, they moved on. These were people that I had never met before in my life. This is the kind of love Jesus expects from all of us.

When I look back now, I believed it was a small test for me from God. He will give you a little test also, just as he tested Abraham as recorded in the book of Genesis, chapter 22. God may not test you to the same degree as Abraham; he may test you with a simple modern problem, as I believe he tested me with the personal story of the pregnant woman and her family. Most of our simple tests from God will come during the time we are waiting for our harvest. Dare to pass your own test!

> When you show love, you are depositing favors in the Bank of heaven.

When you show love, you are also depositing favors in the Bank of Heaven. "One day of God's favor is better than a thousand years of labor." The kind of interest and prosperity that God will in turn reward you with will truly amaze you. This is guaranteed in the mighty name of Jesus Christ.

If you do not give sufficient water to your seed, it is not going to do bear much fruit. Jesus tells us to show love to our sisters, brothers, neighbors, strangers and associates, and he will remain in us and bless us just as Our Lord voiced in the book of John, chapter 15, verses 9-12;

> "As the father has loved me,
> so I have loved you: remain in my love.
> You will remain in my love if you keep my
> Commandments, just as I have kept my
> Father's commandments and remain in his love.
> I have told you all this that my own joy may be in
> you and your joy may be complete. This is my
> Commandment: LOVE ONE ANOTHER AS I
> HAVE LOVED YOU."

When you forgive and love, you will be amazed how much healing and prosperity you will have in your life. Dare to forgive! Dare even more to love!

"We urge you to warn the idle, encourage those who feel discouraged, sustain the weak, and have patience with everyone. See that no one repays evil with evil, whether among yourselves or towards others."...
Apostle Paul (1 Thessalonians 5 v 14-15)

"Constant kindness can accomplish much. As the sun makes ice melt, kindness causes misunderstanding, mistrust, and hostility to evaporate. It is only imperfection that complains of what is imperfect"...Joseph Addison

15

The Power of Patience

I would like to share another family story. When I was about ten years old, my older brother worked for an oil refinery in the Eastern part of Nigeria. One afternoon, while helping my mother with house chores, a close friend brought us disturbing news; an accident had occurred in the refinery where my brother worked, leaving him severely burned and on life support. My mother and I proceeded to the hospital as fast as humanly possible. When we arrived at his hospital bed, we could hardly recognize him due to the severity of the scars covering his body. His degree of burn could not be categorized.

The accident happened when his colleague, who was laying only a few beds away from him, mistakenly lit a cigarette thinking no one was working. The explosion and fire that ensued can be better imagined than described.

The physical pain both men experienced as they struggled to recuperate was unconscionable. Through prayers, immense treatment, and patience, they soon began to recover. After about six months, they both made full recoveries. As I look at my brother today, I am almost in disbelief that he is the same person who was lying in that hospital bed. Aside from a minor scar around his stomach, there remains no trace of this tragic accident.

Most people who have had their heart broken might describe the intensity of their pain as akin to the pain experienced by my brother in his unfortunate accident. Victims of infidelity, rape, or child abuse experience unimaginable emotional and physical pains. Regardless of the type of pain you have endured, following the steps outlined in this book will ultimately lead to your complete healing. You must exercise patience and pray often so that the Holy Spirit may take control. It took six months of treatment and forgiving his colleague for both men to be completely healed. This power of patience can heal you also.

> Patience is essentially the sunlight needed for the growth of a sown seed.

Though you may have some lingering emotional scars, similar to the minor physical scar left on my brother, realize that these scars simply serve as a reminder of a bad path traveled and your broken heart will be made anew.

In regards to prosperity, patience is another key factor or ingredient needed for our seed to grow and bring much fruit. Patience is essentially the sunlight needed for the growth of a sown seed. When you sow your seed, growth is not expected overnight, but rather time is vital to the maturation process. Similarly, when you plant your seed to God, you need to have patience. Patience usually requires steadfastness, and on some occasions suffering and forbearance.

The book of Romans chapter 5 verses 3-5 (amplified version) said;

> "Not only that we feel secure even in
> trials, knowing that trials produce patience,
> from patience comes merit, merit is the source of hope
> and hope does not disappoint us because the Holy spirit
> has been given to us, pouring into our hearts the love of God."

When a seed is implanted into a woman, she becomes pregnant, yet she must wait patiently for nine long months before delivering her baby. During the first two months of pregnancy, it's almost impossible to discern whether a woman is pregnant or not.

A pregnant woman does not want the baby in the first month. She does not want the baby in the second, third or even as late as the seventh month. She wants her baby in the ninth month, after the baby has gone through the entire process and fetus is fully developed. During her nine months of patiently waiting, she experiences all sorts of discomfort, irritability and so forth. Sometimes she feels like she is ready to have the baby before the due time. But she knows she must be patient and pray that the baby stays to complete the process. She is advised to eat well, rest, exercise, and refrain from smoking, drugs and to think less. The bottom line here is that a patient and disciplined mother is rewarded with the harvest of a healthy, bouncing baby.

This is exactly what you need to do while you await your harvest from God. You need to have the patience of a pregnant woman. After you have sown your seed, you must pray at least twice a day. This is our way to communicate with God. You cannot have a proper relationship with anyone without communication. You must continue to exercise childlike forgiveness on a daily basis. You have to continue to love, no matter the circumstance. Study one to two chapters of the bible daily. Stay focus and be kind to people. When you do all these things, and do them well, you will begin to see your harvest within a few months.

In the United States today and in most developed countries, people who have been at a job longer that two years are eligible for a 401 K plan, or some sort of retirement plan such as an IRA. The objective of these plans is to give financial support in one's golden year. The question now is how much have you deposited in your heavenly 401 K or IRA? Our Lord Jesus Christ said in the book Matthew chapter 6 verses 19-20;

> Study one or two chapters of the bible daily. Stay focus and be kind to people.

> "Do not store up treasure for yourself
> on earth where moth and rust destroy it and
> where thieves can steal it. Store up treasure for
> yourself with God, where no moth or rust can destroy
> nor thieves come and steal it."

Have you shown enough forgiveness and love for your name to be written in the book of life? Where do you plan to spend eternity? How many people around you have you forgiven and shown love to lately? Always remember, they key to prosperity, healing or any favor from God, are; FORGIVENESS, LOVE AND PATIENCE. Make up your mind to walk in truth as contained in this book. The power of the Holy Spirit will enable you to achieve this goal and after this short spiritual journey called life, will allow you to spend eternity in Heaven with the Lord.

"If you say, "I love God" while you hate your brother or sister you are a lair. How can you love God whom you do not see, if you do not love your brother whom you see? We received from him this commandment: Let those who love God also love their brothers...Apostle John (1 John 4 v 20)

"The day a child realizes that all adults are imperfect, he becomes an adolescent; the day he forgives them, he becomes an adult; the day he forgives himself, he becomes wise."—Alden Nolan

16

Conclusion—With No Option, Can We Let It Go?

A World View

Throughout this book I have emphasized how forgiveness, love, and patience can significantly improve our lives. These attributes can also be used to heal and open the door for spiritual and global prosperity for everyone around the world. Just about every person around the world, including young children, dream of peace and happiness. We can learn from these children as illustrated in the earlier story involving my then five year old daughter.

Most countries today, possess nuclear weapons which are capable of destroying the world as we know it. Every day we hope and pray that these countries exercises restraint in using these weapons of mass destruction. The possibility of total annihilation has become so engrained in our society that many of us appear to be unconcerned. All it would take for our worst nightmares to come true is a simple command from one demented leader. Life on earth as we know it could become history and it virtually depends on the wisdom and restraint from these few leaders.

> The possibility of total annihilation has become so engrained in our society that many of us appear to be unconcerned.

At any moment these leaders could give the order. What happens when leaders of the terrorist organizations get hold of these weapons? You might say to yourself that is highly improbable, but the horrific events in New York on September 11, 2001 should be a firm reminder.

God, in his infinite mercy, has spared this earth from our evil intentions. Nations must continue with peace negotiations, forgive one another, and dismantle these formidable weapons that threaten our very existence. Our Children, grant Children and generations yet to be born are counting on it.

Numerous unfortunate and senseless murders occur around the world today. Most of us are tired of watching the news everyday only to see our children getting killed by bullets, bomb, starvation, or simple preventable diseases. We must bind together and preach this message of forgiveness and love. Most concerns about forgiveness are inherited not learned. Through prayer and love for one another, starting from the family setting, we can resolve to let go of our ingrained prejudices and bitterness.

> Nations must continue with peace negotiations, forgive one another, and dismantle these formidable weapons that threaten our very existence.

We should pray to God and through his Son, Jesus Christ, who will show us the art of forgiveness. God respects our free will. Unless we pray and give the heavens the permission to intercede, nothing can be done. We should learn to respect those we do least understand and those we hate the most. In order for our society to progress, we must learn to forgive, love, and have patience with one another.

Quotes on Forgiveness

Mahatma Gandhi

The weak can never forgive. Forgiveness is the attribute of the strong.

To forgive is to set a prisoner free and discover the prisoner was YOU

Josh Billings

There is no revenge as complete as forgiveness.

Forgiveness is the economy of the heart…Forgiveness saves expense of anger, the cost of hatred, the waste of spirits.

Hannah MOR

As long as you don't forgive, who and whatever it will occupy rent-free space in your mind…

Constant kindness can accomplish much. As the sun makes ice melt, kindness causes misunderstanding, mistrust, and hostility to evaporate. It is only imperfection that complains of what is imperfect. The more perfect we are, wards the defects of the gentler and quiet we become to others.— **Joseph Addison.**

Most of our suspicions by our knowledge of ourselves.

You cannot antagonize and influence at the same time.—**J. S. Knox.**

The very purpose of existence is to reconcile the glowing opinion we hold of ourselves with the appalling things that other people think about us.— **Quentin Crisp.**

Suggested Readings

Casarjian, Robin. Forgiveness: A Bold Choice for a Peaceful Heart, New York; Bantam Books, 1992

Childre, Doc Lew; Howard, Beech, Donna. The Heartmath Solution, Haper San Francisco, New York, New York, 2000

Enright, Robert D Forgiveness Is a Choice, Washington, D.C; APA Life Tools, 2001

Enright, Robert D, and Joanna North, Eds; Exploring Forgiveness, Madison; University of Wisconsin Press, 1998

Hallowell, Edward. Dare To Forgive, Deerfield Beach, Health Communications, 2004

Karen, Robert. The Forgiving Self: The Road from Resentment to Connection, New York; Doubleday, 2001.

Lieberman, David J. Make Peace with Anyone, New York: St Martin's Press 2002

Luskin, Fred. Forgive for Good, San Francisco; HaperSanFrisco, 2002

Meier, Paul, and Minirth Frank, Md. Happiness is a Choice; Grand Rapids, Baker book, 2002

Smedes, Lewis B. The Art of Forgiving, New York; Ballantine Books, 1996

Yancey, Philip. What So Amazing About Grace; Zondervan Publishing, 2002

Warren, Rick. The Purpose Driven Life; Zondervan Publishing, 2002

Worthington, Everett L, ed. Dimensions of forgiveness: Psychological Research and Theological Perspectives. Radnor, Pa: Templeton Foundation Press, 1998

About the Author

Elu Akpala Onnekikami (PhD) is the Co-founder of World Christians Bread of Life Ministries, which is headquartered in Victorville California. He is an Evangelist, motivational and Inspirational speaker in immense demand around the globe. Thousands have come to his open air crusades, pastoral and business conferences around the world.

To obtain additional information on seminars, to schedule speaking engagements, or to write the author with your personal inspirational stories on forgiveness, Love, faith, general comments or Prayer requests, please address your correspondence to:

> World Christians Bread of life Ministries
> P. O Box 2098
> Victorville, CA 92393
> USA

You may also reach him via e-mail: dr.elu@worldchristiansonline.org or visit the ministry website for additional information: www.worldchristiansonline.org

978-0-595-37878-4
0-595-37878-1

Printed in the United States
66793LVS00003BA/34-42